POETRY from Crescent Moon Publishing

Peter Redgrove: Here Comes the Flood
by Jeremy Mark Robinson

Walking In Cornwall
Ursula Le Guin

Arthur Rimbaud: *Selected Poems*
edited and translated by Andrew Jary

Arthur Rimbaud: *A Season in Hell*
edited and translated by Andrew Jary

Friedrich Hölderlin: *Hölderlin's Songs of Light: Selected Poems*
translated by Michael Hamburger

Rainer Maria Rilke: *Dance the Orange: Selected Poems*
translated by Michael Hamburger

Arseny Tarkovsky: *Life, Life: Selected Poems*
translated by Virginia Rounding

Brigitte's Blue Heart
by Jeremy Reed

Claudia Schiffer's Red Shoes
by Jeremy Reed

By-Blows: Uncollected Poems
by D.J. Enright

William Shakespeare: *Selected Sonnets and Verse*
edited, with an introduction by Mark Tuley

Edmund Spenser: *Poems*
selected and introduced by Teresa Page

Robert Herrick: *Selected Poems*
edited and introduced by M.K. Pace

Sir Thomas Wyatt: *Poems*
selected and introduced by Louise Cooper

John Donne: *Poems*
selected and introduced by A.H. Ninham

D.H. Lawrence: *Selected Poems*
edited with an introduction by Margaret Elvy

Percy Bysshe Shelley: *Poems*
selected and introduced by Charlotte Greene

Thomas Hardy: *Selected Poems*
edited, with an introduction by A.H. Ninham

Emily Bronte: *Poems*
selected and introduced by Teresa Page

John Keats: *Selected Poems*
edited with an introduction by Miriam Chalk

Henry Vaughan: *Poems*
selected and introduced by A.H. Ninham

The Crescent Moon Book of Love Poetry
edited by Louise Cooper

The Crescent Moon Book of Mystical Poetry in English
edited by Carol Appleby

The Crescent Moon Book of Nature Poetry From Langland to Lawrence
edited by Margaret Elvy

The Crescent Moon Book of Metaphysical Poetry
edited and introduced by Charlotte Greene

The Crescent Moon Book of Elizabethan Love Poetry
edited and introduced by Carol Appleby

The Crescent Moon Book of Romantic Poetry
edited and introduced by L.M. Poole

Blinded By Her Light The Love-Poetry of Robert Graves
by Jeremy Mark Robinson

*Shakespeare: Love, Poetry and Magic
in Shakespeare's Sonnets and Plays*
by B.D. Barnacle

*German Romantic Poetry: Goethe, Novalis,
Heine, Hölderlin, Schlegel, Schiller*
by Carol Appleby

Cavafy: Anatomy of a Soul
by Matt Crispin

Rilke: Space, Essence and Angels in the Poetry of Rainer Maria Rilke
by B.D. Barnacle

Rimbaud: Arthur Rimbaud and the Magic of Poetry
by Jeremy Mark Robinson

Petrarch, Dante and the Troubadours: The Religion of Love and Poetry
by Cassidy Hughes

Dante: *Selections From the Vita Nuova*
translated by Thomas Okey

Jeremy Robinson has written many critical studies, including *Hayao Miyazaki, Walerian Borowczyk, Arthur Rimbaud,* and *The Sacred Cinema of Andrei Tarkovsky*, plus literary monographs on: Shakespeare; Samuel Beckett; Thomas Hardy; André Gide; Robert Graves; and John Cowper Powys.

It's amazing for me to see my work treated with such passion and respect. There is nothing resembling it in the U.S. in relation to my work.

Andrea Dworkin (on *Andrea Dworkin*)

This model monograph – it is an exemplary job, and I'm very proud that he has accorded me a couple of mentions... The subject matter of his book is beautifully organised and dead on beam.

Lawrence Durrell (on *The Light Eternal: A Study of J.M.W. Turner*)

His poetry is very good deep moving stuff.

Cloud Nine magazine

Jeremy Robinson's poetry is certainly jammed with ideas, and I find it very interesting for that reason. It's certainly a strong imprint of his personality.

Colin Wilson

Sex-Magic-Poetry-Cornwall is a very rich essay... It is a very good piece... vastly stimulating and insightful.

Peter Redgrove

Sex-Magic-Poetry-Cornwall

The Poems of Peter Redgrove

Sex-Magic-Poetry-Cornwall

The Poems of Peter Redgrove

Jeremy Mark Robinson

CRESCENT MOON

Crescent Moon Publishing
P.O. Box 393
Maidstone
Kent
ME14 5XU, U.K.

First published April 6, 1994
Poems © Peter Redgrove 1994
Essay © Jeremy Mark Robinson 1994
Revised edition September 11, 1995
Poems © Peter Redgrove 1995
Essay © Jeremy Mark Robinson 1995
3rd edition 2007
Poems © Peter Redgrove 2007
Essay © Jeremy Mark Robinson 2007
4th edition 2011

Printed and bound in the U.S.A.
Set in Bodoni Book and Gills Sans Light 10 on 14pt.
Designed by Radiance Graphics.

The right of Jeremy Mark Robinson to be identified as the author of *Sex-Magic-Poetry-Cornwall* has been asserted generally in accordance with sections 77 and 78 of the Copyright, Designs and Patents Act 1988.

All rights reserved. No part of this book may be reprinted or reproduced, stored in a retrieval system, or transmitted, in any form or by any means, electronic, mechanical, photocopying, recording or otherwise, without permission from the publisher.

British Library Cataloguing in Publication data

Robinson, Jeremy Mark
Sex-Magic-Poetry-Cornwall: The Poems of Peter Redgrove
I. Title
821.914

ISBN-13 9781861712950

CONTENTS

Acknowledgements   *11*
Abbreviations   *13*
Preface To the 3rd Edition   *21*
Preface To the New Edition   *23*

One   *The Outer and Inner Life*   *29*
Two   *Alchemy of the Word : Redgrove's Poetics*   *39*
Three   *Adventures in the Mother-World :*
            Extra-Sensuous Perception   *67*
Four   *The Goddess and Feminism*   *99*
Five   *Sex Magic, Sex Alchemy, Sex Yoga*   *119*
Six   *A Critical Appraisal of Peter Redgrove's Poetry*   *129*

Illustrations   *133*
Notes   *151*
Bibliography   *161*

ACKNOWLEDGEMENTS

Thanks to Peter Redgrove.

COPYRIGHT HOLDERS

The Collector and Other Poems, Routledge & Kegan Paul 1959 [hereafter cited as RKP]; *The Nature of Cold Weather and Other Poems*, RKP, 1961; *At the White Monument and Other Poems*, RKP, 1963; *The Force and Other Poems*, RKP, 1966; *Work in Progress*, Poet & Printer, 1969; *Dr Faust's Sea-Spiral Spirit and Other Poems*, RKP, 1972; *In the Country of the Skin: A Radio Script*, Peter Redgrove, Falmouth, 1973; *Three Pieces For Voices*, Poet and Printer, 1973; *From Every Chink of the Ark and other new poems*, RKP, 1977; *Happiness*, Priapus, 1978; *The Weddings at Nether Powers and other new poems*, RKP, 1979; *The God of Glass*, RKP, 1979; *The Beekeepers*, RKP, 1980; *The Apple-Broadcast and other new poems*, RKP, 1981; *The Working of Water*, Taxus Press, 1984; *The Man Named East and other new poems*, RKP, 1985; *The Mudlark Poems*, Rivelin Grapheme Press, 1986; *In the Hall of the Saurians*, Secker & Warburg, 1987; *Poems 1954-1987*, Penguin, 1989; *The First Earthquake*, Secker & Warburg, 1989; *Sulfur*, 1989, 1991; *Margin* no. 10; *Ambit; Manhattan Review*, 1990/ 95; *Poetry USA*, 1992; *Dressed As For a Tarot Pack*, Taxus, 1990; *Under the Reservoir*, Secker & Warburg, 1992; *The Laborators*, Stride, 1993; *The Cyclopean Mistress*, Bloodaxe Books, 1993; *My Father's Trapdoors*, Cape, 1994; *Abyssophone*, Stride, 1995; *Assembling a Ghost*, Cape, 1996; *Orchard End*, Stride, 1997; *What the Black Mirror Saw*, Stride, 1997; *From the Virgin Caverns*, Cape, 2002; *Sheen*, Stride, 2003; *A Speaker For the Silver Goddess*, Stride, 2006.

PICTURE CREDITS

British Library for illustrations from *The Mirror of Alchemy*, British Library, 1994.
Ana Mendieta. Niki de Sant-Phalle. Eric Gill.
Joe Arthurs, 2006.
All other images by Jeremy Mark Robinson, 1996-2010.

ABBREVIATIONS

SS	"Scientist of the Strange", interview
Laz	"Lazarus and the Visionary Truth", interview
NCW	*The Nature of Cold Weather and Other Poems*
WM	*At the White Monument*
For	*The Force*
Dr	*Dr Faust's Sea-Spiral Spirit*
ICS	*In the Country of the Skin*
Ark	*From Every Chink of the Ark*
WNP	*The Weddings at Nether Powers*
AB	*The Apple-Broadcast*
WW	*The Working of Water*
Man	*The Man Named East*
Mud	*The Mudlark Poems*
IHS	*In the Hall of the Saurians*
Sel	*Poems 1954-1987*
FE	*The First Earthquake*
Tar	*Dressed As For a Tarot Pack*
UR	*Under the Reservoir*
Lab	*The Laborators*
Ab	*Abyssophone*
OE	*Orchard End*
FVC	*From the Virgil Caverns*
BG	*The Black Goddess and the Sixth Sense*
AFW	*Alchemy For Women*
CIT	*A Crystal of Industrial Time*
AJ	*An Alchemical Journal*

BEES AT LAND'S END

Music comes, a giant's hum from below the sea-line,
Clanging of cliffs rocked with a salty hiss
Leaping out from the crack of a rounded stone
Where light pours crystalline, in liquid granite,
Bouncing onto blue sea-washed calcite.

An aeroplane murmurs above, banking
For Sennen Cove and Land's End aerodrome.
The sound comes deeper now, but it's not
The arcade screech of a million fruit machines
That make Penzance glitter like Las Vegas.

It's not the whine of pylons in a high wind,
Or the limpid song of a star-bound lark.
No, the sound's in the belly, in the plexus,
It's boulders rolling on the sea bed, heard
In the out-lying tunnel of a mine.

Falling in crashes, the waves rock our bodies,
Billowed out, wet, full as a galleon's sail,
And drenched in the blood of fantasy pirates,
We voyagers on the high seas of the soul,
Treasure chests spilled open on booming canvas.

Sea on all sides, like being in a mirror,
The blue-on-blue of sea and sky, sea and sky,
With the sun sewn under our skin in a pouch
Which expands and illuminates the body
So all's warmth and again the taste of salt.

The whisper now of pampas grass and strange plants,
The twin paths that snake below the steep slopes,
The gulleys open up sudden and vicious,
You could fall, knowing nothing for seconds,
Then... the impact with rock or water - nirvana.

Still the sound swells, as you enter the farm.
Goats with pink eyes, wood, straw, cream teas, chickens,
And a marvellous glass honey bee hive,
The bees at work in the honeycomb city,
The Queen Bee marked by a white spot on her back.

Here's where the music rises, this bee hive,
The sound rolls out over all of Cornwall,
The choiring of celestial angels, the bees,
They're so small, yet so loud, antenna tuned in
To the global broadcast of the ocean.

Jeremy Mark Robinson

Written after a visit to Peter Redgrove in Cornwall, 1993.

Everything can become magical-work.

Novalis *(Pollen)*

A postcard from Peter Redgrove (of May 13, 1993), showing Glendurgan Garden, near Falmouth and its famous maze (National Trust).

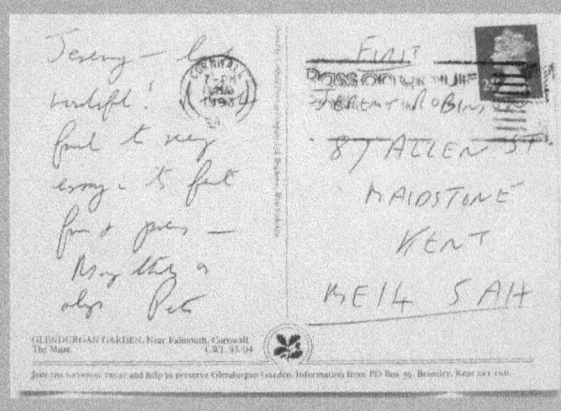

Preface To the 3rd Edition

This third edition of *Sex-Magic-Poetry-Cornwall* has been published in the wake of Peter Redgrove's death in 2003. The aim of this selection of Peter Redgrove's poetry is to collect together some of his most intense pieces as well as representative works. Many poets are little dribbles of water. Peter Redgrove, like D.H. Lawrence or Arthur Rimbaud, is a river, a waterfall, a flood. The poet Kathleen Raine said that reading Redgrove 's poetry is 'like standing under a waterfall in full spate'. So reading these poems you will hopefully get wet – very wet. Soaked through, if possible.

The essay reviews all Peter Redgrove's poetry, and many of his key ideas. This collection originally opened with three shamanic poems which conjure up storms, rain, lightning, thunder and floods – recurring motifs in Redgrove's poetry. Other poems focus on love and eroticism, and the Cornish landscape, and these three things – love; magic/ yoga/ shamanism; and Cornwall/ nature/ landscape – recur throughout Redgrove's work, and throughout this 'flood' of poems. There are also groups of witchy and magical poems; poems about the Lizard and Goonhilly; poems about waterworks; poems about larking around in mud; and Redgrove's notion of 'extra sensuous perception'.

Peter Redgrove's contemporaries, such as Ted Hughes and Sylvia Plath, have become celebrated, while Redgrove has unfortunately remained something of a cult poet, with a much smaller (though dedicated) following. As these poems show, Redgrove deserves to be fêted as the equal of the greatest of poets of the 20th century, alongside British poets such as Robert Graves, W.B. Yeats, W.H. Auden and Ted Hughes.

For this third edition, the essay has been completely rewritten.

I would like to thank Peter Redgrove.

Jeremy Mark Robinson
Kent, England, 2007

Preface For the New Edition

For this edition of *Peter Redgrove: Here Comes the Flood*, we cannot print whole poems by Peter Redgrove (due to the people who control Redgrove's estate).

This is a pity, partly because Redgrove had been delighted by the approach I had taken to his work. We corresponded often about this book and the two companion books. Here is a selection of Redgrove's letters to me:

> Thanks very much for your exciting draft. I'm of course very glad that you feel the poems sustain and feed back the vision you describe... Some of your phrases were personally helpful to me... What you write becomes a great rush of invocation and suggestion – as I say, I'm glad that the poems stand up in the force of your (ever welcome) enthusiasm... It is very good for me that the *Alchemical Journal* works as it does on you – there is that shock of recognition which the imagination is prone to languish...
>
> This is a very rich essay you have written... I greatly look forward to seeing it in its final form – it is very energising for me to have your

response to this work – poems that I thought had closed are opening again! ...I hope I have written enough to show how appreciate I am of your voracious reading and your response.

Peter Redgrove, April 14, 1993

Your essay has an infectious enthusiasm, which I'm grateful for, and I especially like the places where you actually grapple with the language of my poems, which is like writing them again. It is a very good piece, which carries the reader with it... Your own approach is irreplaceable because it seems to us founded on your own individuality and personal experience of my poems – which is vastly gratifying... in the majority it is vastly stimulating and insightful. Always, I am grateful to you for your trouble, and your deep response to what I have written.

Peter Redgrove, letter, May 19, 1993

Very many thanks for 'Our Book' which I shall always treasure. It is like a brightly-lighted box in which you have turned on all the light of your enthusiasm, so that the poems glow like the calcite of the underground rocks do in the ultra-violet of the poem in the Esplumeor sequence... This is spooky for me since the poems have resurrected themselves – there is usually so little feedback that one cannot believe one has written something that one knew one was writing them, until the circuit is closed again and the current flows... It was a good idea of yours to use the image of the waterfall beating on the head of the poet or the reader... There is a right emphasis on ecstasy – that is indeed the point.

I don't think anybody has said this before, I think you have chosen the poems well, and written well about them. Thank you! I shall always be grateful... It is wonderful to see the poems responding to your insights. Penelope [Shuttle] says that your readings of the individual

SEX–MAGIC–POETRY–CORNWALL

texts in your essay are among the best she has seen anywhere.

I like very much the way you have resurrected poems I had forgotten worked, like the clothes magic-wet and the alchemical honeymoon – I thought they didn't work because nobody had put them in context before of the elemental life that nudges into them always – and I like the cragginess of the prose poems in contrast. Your choice of quotations is excellent throughout, and this is the real point – plus enthusiasm... it is like a laser gas into which you pump your enthusiastic energy, there is a sudden shift of atomic orbits, and the texts shine with their own weird and natural light!

Peter Redgrove, letter, November 7, 1993

Peter Redgrove was a wonderful collaborator, exchanging so many letters and ideas, sending me many books, pamphlets and interviews, and explaining his themes, images and poems in detail.

Jeremy Mark Robinson
Kent, England, 2011

Sex–Magic–Poetry–Cornwall

The Poems of Peter Redgrove

I

The Outer and Inner Biography

1.1   Life / Influences / Context

> There are few men of such range of personality, human learning and understanding and zest for life. He is the most prolific poet of the last twenty years and one of the most enigmatic. He writes of everything.
>
> Martin Booth (227)

Peter Redgrove's life has been well-documented elsewhere, in his many interviews, as well as studies, so I won't explore it at length here.[1] Born in Kingston-upon-Thames, Surrey, in 1932, he went from public school to Cambridge University to read natural sciences. Redgrove worked as a scientist, a copywriter, and also taught at Falmouth College of Art for years (as well as in Buffalo and Leeds). He married Barbara

SEX–MAGIC–POETRY–CORNWALL

Sherlock, a sculptor, in 1954; they had two children. Redgrove's second wife was poet Penelope Shuttle (they had a daughter, Zoe). He spent much of his later life in Cornwall.

Peter Redgrove was part of the Group poets, and is placed by critics in the Ted Hughes-Sylvia Plath-Philip Hobsbaum circle of poets. He spoke warmly of Ted Hughes, but says his poetry is quite different.[2] Indeed, Hughes and Redgrove are in some respects very different poets. They both use the same formal elements like the three line stanza that Sylvia Plath employed so powerfully (in her famous 'Lady Lazarus', for example). But the imagery, goals, allusions and outlook of Hughes and Redgrove are quite different. There are plenty of affinities, though: the nature mysticism, the sensuality and earthiness, the visionary elements, the Romanticism, the Jungian psychology (and Hughes even wrote of the Goddess in his later work). Both Redgrove and Hughes believed in the physicality of language, how words could becomes real experiences.

Ted Hughes's poetic world, for instance, is out of William Shakespeare in *King Lear,* with all that wind, rain, barren earth, darkness/ light, craggy hills and tormented psyche toppling over in the void inside itself. Rather as if the Welsh/ Harlech green world of Robert Graves had been re-shot by Ingmar Bergman at the height of his *The Virgin Spring* period.

Peter Redgrove I have sometimes felt recalls the novelist J.G. Ballard (born in 1930, Ballard is, like Ted Hughes, Redgrove's contemporary). There is the same idiosyncratic and often bizarre way of experiencing the world. Ballard will speak of the volumes of air inverting themselves behind someone as they move in a room (in his *The Atrocity Exhibition*, for example).[3] Like Ballard and Hughes, Redgrove also employed heaps of shamanism, post-Jungian psychology and Western mythology. Redgrove may not like to be associated with Ballard's ruthless and self-conscious postmodernism, but this extract from the poem 'The Silvery Old Goldsmith' shows just how Ballardian Redgrove could be, or how Redgrovean Ballard is: the goldsmith, a shamanic and alchemical figure, has made a construction which is

> a tree of spikes of silver
> Set in ebony, say two feet high;
> It was white lightning branching within
> Jet thunder, done
> As a midget's hat-stand: 'It is a model
> To scale of a radio-echo engraving on the sky
> For a split-second all of Chopin's
> Funeral march in the one figure.' (UR, 25)

That's a very Ballardian image. Both Ballard and Redgrove liked to take modern science and consider it from a visionary and poetic viewpoint. When Redgrove looked at an orchard, for example, he didn't see a bunch of trees and grass, or even the blossom and fruit of the ordinary poet, but complex natural phenomena which were interlinked and multi-layered, with their own beauty (like wasps and bees, for instance, in poems such as 'Orchard With Wasps').

Among poetic influences, which are worth little really, and only form what I've called here the 'outside' biography, Redgrove cited William Langland, T.S. Eliot, Robert Frost, Edward Thomas and Samuel Taylor Coleridge. He admired 'Shakespeare for his eloquence', not for his worldview or his 'atmosphere'.[4] He appreciated the thoroughly patriarchal *Bible* for its poetic magic, but not for its morality. He said he was not influenced by Robert Graves or D.H. Lawrence, but the similarities with his poetry are many in both Graves and Lawrence.

D.H. Lawrence, for instance, wrote in his short stories (and in many others places) of the touch that awakens life. In "A Propos of *Lady Chatterley's Lover*", Lawrence wrote: '[w]e must get back into relation, vivid and nourishing relation to the cosmos'.[5] The basic thrust of Lorenzo's philosophy was the struggle into being, into awareness, into a direct relation, or touch, with people and the world. Redgrove's aims, as will be seen, are similar.

Though known primarily as a poet, Peter Redgrove also wrote novels, plays (many performed on BBC radio), articles, and non-fiction studies (such as the trilogy *The Wise Wound*, *The Black Goddess and the Sixth Sense* and *Alchemy For Women* – two of those were co-written with Penelope Shuttle). All of these works fed into each other: Redgrove's short stories were adapted as radio plays (or vice versa), many poems were incorporated into the novels, and the insights in the psychological studies drew on the poetry.

The medium of radio, for instance, was important for Redgrove: his poems often explore radio waves, broadcasts and sounds. And radio provided metaphors and analogies: sounds moving out into the world like scents, for instance. And Redgrove's radio plays were quite different from anything being broadcast at the time. They were instantly recognizable as the work of Peter Redgrove with their references to altered states, extra-sensuous perception, hypnotism, folk traditions, Cornwall and eroticism.

1.2   Psychology / Poetics

What this amounts to is a misleading, external biography, a lineage which is not really useful for approaching the real Peter Redgrove. Far more important have been the magical, mythical, psychological and emotional influences. His biggest influence, and the centre of his poetic world, was his second wife, Penelope Shuttle. 'The greatest influence is undoubtedly Penelope Shuttle,' he wrote to me.[1]

'Experiences' is a far better term than 'influences', for Redgrove everywhere emphasies the 'experienced'. That is, life as lived in the body, in the flesh, not in the abstract or literary sense.

Redgrove's secret or interior lineage stems from C.G. Jung, John Layard and Gerald Massey among thinkers.[2] It is possible, for instance, to analyze Redgrove's poesie from a purely Jungian standpoint and get very close to its essence. Alternatively, one might fruitfully look at Redgrove in terms of feminism, which I do later on. Or in terms of (the history of) magic. Or New Age/ self-help/ Mind, Body, Spirit thinking. Or the natural sciences. All these strains link up in the Redgroverse (Redgrove's multiverse), while the great unifier is of course the poet himself.

Some of the writers and philosophers and the books they wrote that Peter Redgrove admired and often referred to included: Elizabeth Sewell's *The Orphic Voice*, a wonderful book about visionary poetry; the *Collected Works* of C.G. Jung's (Jung's influence on Redgrove's thinking can be found everywhere; Jung probably influenced more artists and writers than Sigmund Freud or Friedrich Nietzsche); J.G. Frazer's *The Golden Bough*, a key sourcebook on mythologies; Joseph Campbell, a more recent writer on world mythology, author of books on the one myth or primal or monomyth such as *The Hero With a Thousand Faces* and *The Masks of God* (Campbell was the darling of the New Hollywood filmmakers, like George Lucas and George Miller); John Layard, a Jungian analyst (author of *The Lady of the Hare*, *The Virgin Archetype* and *A Celtic Quest*); Barbara Walker, a US feminist writer on women's magic and the Goddess (she wrote *The Women's Encyclopedia of Myths ad Secrets*; Mary Daly, a more strident feminist on religion, was another reference point); earlier writers on the Goddess, such as Robert Briffault and his book *The Mothers*, or Erich Neumann and *The Great Mother*; Robert Graves's *The White Goddess* and *Mammon and the Black Goddess*; M. Esther Harding's *Women's Mysteries*; Chris Knight's *Blood Relations* (I remember discussing Knight's 1991 book on menstruation in early cultures at length with Redgrove in the early Nineties); Alex Comfort, famous as the author of *The Joy of Sex* and *More Joy of Sex*; James Hillman (author of *The Dream and the Underworld*); Kenneth Grant, who wrote many books on magic(ke); Bruno Bettelheim, the Jungian writer on fairy tales and psychology; Gerald Massey, the 19th century mythographer and poet (cited many times in *The Black Goddess and the Sixth Sense*); and theologian Paul Tillich.

SEX–MAGIC–POETRY–CORNWALL

Redgrove also cited writers on Oriental philosophy, sexual yoga and Taoist sexual practices, such as Mantak Chia (*Taoist Secrets of Love*), Philip Rawson (*The Art of Tantra*), and Stephen Chang (*Chinese Yoga*). And Western studies of psychology and sexuality, such as those of Sigmund Freud, H.J. Eysenck, Claude Lévi-Strauss, Masters and Johnson, Havelock Ellis, Charles Tart, Georg Groddeck, Otto Rank, and R.D. Laing. Redgrove was also interested in the experiments in altered states, hypnosis and magic, of people such as Anton Mesmer, A.E. Waite, Aleister Crowley and the Golden Dawn. And writers on scientific matters , such as Fred Hoyle, William Thomson, and A.N. Whitehead. Among feminist writers, Redgrove and Shuttle cited people like Sheila Kitzinger, Barbara Walker, Mary Daly, and Simone de Beauvoir.

You'll find these writers and books cited in the bibliographies of *The Wise Wound, The Black Goddess and the Sixth Sense* and *Alchemy For Women*. It's clear that Peter Redgrove had these authors and their books close at hand when he was writing his non-fiction and articles.

In my conversations with Peter Redgrove, we'd talk about Georg Groddeck, Johann Wolfgang von Goethe, Novalis, Aleister Crowley, Sigmund Freud and of course C.G. Jung. I'd bring in people like Lawrence Durrell, Henry Miller, John Cowper Powys, and D.H. Lawrence (he wasn't that keen on Durrell or – perhaps surprisingly – Lorenzo, but he loved Powys, and often referred to that moment in Powys's *Autobiography* where J.C.P goes into ecstasy at the sight of moss on a wall. We also discussed G. Wilson Knight's appraisal of the anal or excremental mysticism in Powys's fiction, which appears in *A Glastonbury Romance* and *Porius*, among other novels).

Georg Groddeck Redgrove liked for his theories on menstruation (it was the best time to make love, Groddeck asserted, with menstrual blood recalling the first thing babies smell and taste. And menstruation is a vital experience, which both men and women can learn from [WW, 73f]). Redgrove cited Groddeck's memory of bathing with his mother as a child when she menstruating, and he saw the black, the white and the red (the colours of alchemy): black pubic hair, white skin and red blood (WW, 245).

I wonder if Peter Redgrove wasn't keen on certain writers because their fields of exploration were so close to his own. Another writer who lived very near to Redgrove, for instance – Colin Wilson (who lived in Gorran Haven, not far from Falmouth) – is notably absent from Redgrove's writings. Similarly with D.H. Lawrence or Ted Hughes.

1.3   Nature / Mysticism / Cornwall

Some critics see Peter Redgrove as a nature mystic. Certainly, there is an amazingly powerful and elemental sense of the natural world in his works. We might cite British poets such as George Herbert, William Shakespeare, Henry Vaughan, William Blake and William Wordsworth as precursors of Redgrovean nature mysticism – these poets (from the Elizabethans through the Metaphysical poets to the Romantics) are behind the poetry of Ted Hughes too, as they form the backbone of the British nature poetry tradition.

Redgrove diverges from nature mystics in their pantheist doctrine of God-in-nature, as espoused by mystics such as Meister Eckhart, John Smith, Richard Jeffries and William Wordsworth. The mystic Jacob Boehme is typical of the pantheic view when writes: '[i]n this light my spirit saw through all things and into all creatures, and I recognized God in grass and plants.'[1]

For Redgrove, the natural world is so extraordinary, it doesn't require a deity or religion to make it extraordinary. It already is extraordinary, and nature doesn't need God to make it like that. At the same time, there is a religious aspect to Redgrove's art, for he exalts the Goddess, as Robert Graves and other poets have done. Redgrove goes for the Black Goddess, the dark side of the deity, but the deification is none the less powerful and spiritual as it is in mediæval mystics. (There is animism, too, in Redgrove's poetry, and shamanism; animism is the basis of all religion, and lies behind shamanism too).

The Duchy exerts a powerful influence on Redgrove. His poems display many aspects of Cornwall in them, not only in obvious ways (in 'Falmouth Clouds' or 'Cornwall Honeymoon'), but also in so much of the imagery, the feelings and the underlife of magic.

Cornwall continued to feature prominently in Redgrove's verse up until his death in 2003. In 2002's *From the Virgil Caverns*, for instance, many of the poems have Cornish settings: 'Sea Visit', 'Elderhouse' (Falmouth), 'Cornwall Mud', 'Lawn Sprinkler and Lighthouse' (the Lizard), 'The Good Old Woman' (Trerice), 'Sleepers' Beach' (Perranporth), and 'A Walk By the Helston Ponds'.

Penelope Shuttle has spoken of three things important in her relationship with Redgrove: love, poetry and Cornwall (which I've suggested in the title of this book: *Sex-Magic-Poetry-Cornwall*),[2] and Cornwall is crucial in Redgrove's poetic world. It is the Cornwall of constantly changing weather, of clouds and storms and bees and orchards and estuaries and mud-flats and mines and stone walls and granite and megaliths and dunes and, of course, the sea, always the sea, on all sides. Redgrove calls it 'the dreaming sea', in so many poems, and of course it is the restless human unconscious *par excellence* (and it feeds his poetry endlessly).

The Alchemical Journal (later published in *The Cyclopean Mistress*) is particularly deeply soaked in Cornish imagery and experiences. In no. 33, Redgrove describes one of the many Cornish mines, near Helston (it's open to the public). Mines, and their glittering minerals, feature a good deal in Redgrove's poetry (in 'Minerals of Cornwall, Stones of Cornwall', for example, or 'Commander of Parasyn'). 'Metals are alive like ourselves' Redgrove wrote in 'A Forest of Invisibles' (CM, 109). In the 'womb' of the Earth, to use an age-old poetic metaphor, alchemical transformations can occur. Redgrove's *Alchemical Journal* is a pæan to the fecundity of the Earth, embodied in the dark spaces of the mines.

Redgrove loves underground spaces – underneath houses, underneath fields, underneath everywhere (the more Freudian, uterine and womb-like the better). Indeed, few contemporary poets have written so often of what lies beneath the visible world. Redgrove is the only poet I know of who has written of the beds of rock underneath a field of wheat, for instance. While a Romantic poet such as John Keats might wax lyrical about crops, harvest and the seasons, the Redgrove-poet is down amongst the geological strata, below the fields. And deeper than that, he's also relating the layers of stone to his lover, and women's ability to 'see' down to those lightless regions because of the 'mirror of blood' of their menstruation.

Redgrove is very fond of limestone caverns (in Wales and other spots), of underground waterworks, of tunnels, cellars and basements. One his last poetry books, *From the Virgil Cavern* (2002), contained a series of poems about limestone caverns. 'We are miners in the dark, | of extraordinary jewels' Redgrove wrote in 'Commander of Parasyn (OE, 57). In those black underground spaces, the scents of rain have colours, and the air itself can be 'tinctured with invisible colours' (OE, 56).

2

Alchemy of the Word: Peter Redgrove's Poetics

2.1 Rilke, Rimbaud, the Romantics and Redgrove

If I place Peter Redgrove into a poetic tradition, it is that of the Romantics, first of all, and the German Romantics in particular: Johann Wolfgang von Goethe especially, and Novalis (the Novalis of *Hymns to the Night*), and not forgetting the powerhouse of German Romantic poetry, Friedrich Hölderlin. Novalis has some wonderful things to say about poetry (collected together in *Pollen*, a terrific poetic handbook), such as '[a]ll must become nourishment... Everything can become magical-work.'[1] Of course everything can – should – become magical-work, and Novalis' magical view of life is that of Redgrove, for whom life is extraordinary – if people are attuned to experiencing it that way.

SEX–MAGIC–POETRY–CORNWALL

RILKE. The poet who sums up the essence of German Romanticism in the 20th century, Rainer Maria Rilke, is a key poet in Redgrove's poetics (for me, Rilke is a far greater poet, more important and more enriching, than the 20th century poets usually trotted out as the height of the British tradition, such as W.H. Auden, T.S. Eliot, W.B. Yeats, Samuel Beckett, etc). So many of Redgrove's ideas chime with those of Rilke's, too many to discuss in detail here. The notion of a vast inner world, for instance, is crucial to Rilke and Redgrove. It is what they found their poetry on.

For Rainer Maria Rilke, poetry is a means of exploring and activating this inner space. So Rilke speaks continually in terms of 'Kunst-Ding' (the 'thing-in-itself' of Existential philosophy), of 'essence', space and darkness (the philosophy of innerness and isness outlined in his *Neue Gedichte*). In Rilke's poesie, just as in Peter Redgrove's, everything is expanding – but not outside, *inside*, in those dark, windy spaces populated by the Rilkean Angel, that marvellous being which achieved the shamanic journey of moving between this world and the invisible world.

Rainer Maria Rilke took his poetics largely from the Symbolist poets – from Stéphane Mallarmé in particular, Paul Verlaine and from his friend Paul Valéry. For Mallarmé, words were Prosperoan magic stuff for achieving a musical solidification of the mysterious invisible. Verlaine and Mallarmé emphasized the concreteness of words, as did Karl Kraus and Ludwig Wittgenstein (albeit in a different way). Redgrove too stresses the *actuality* of his poetry, the very feel of lines and rhythms. Looking at the poems here, one might think they tend towards prose, which is true. But each line is carefully worked out, even so. As Eva Salzman admitted: 'I, for one, forgive him his excesses; in fact, I positively love them.'

Rainer Maria Rilke developed Mallarmé's ideas, writing: '[a] poem enters into language from within... It fills the language wondrously, rising to its very brim'.[2] Like Redgrove, Rilke believed in the supernatural power of poetry to grasp the synæsthetic experiences of life.[3]

SEX–MAGIC–POETRY–CORNWALL

Redgrove called this magical apprehension natural, not supernatural, which is his strength, noted Pascale Petit. Redgrove's 'celebratory materialism' is problematic for some (D. Kennedy, 90), while others claim his 'singing materialism' is 'ultimately optimistic' (B. O'Donoghue). Redgrove is fully in accord with Rilke when the German poet writes in his marvellous *Sonnets to Orpheus*:[4]

> What infinity!
> Can't you feel inside your mouth a growing
> mysteriousness, and, where words were, a flowing
> of suddenly released discovery?

This mystical expansion, of fruit inside the mouth, is something Redgrove can relate to, because his poetry works on this concrete, fleshly level. Rilke's sense of space is unparalleled in poetry (see his 'The Bowl of Roses', for instance, which talks so lyrically about the self-illumined Within).[5]

Peter Redgrove is a firm believer in the fundamentally magical aspect of poetry, its ability to conjure up experiences, so that the poem becomes an *experience in itself*, not simply a *description* of an experience. This is a key ethic in post-Symbolist poetics: that the poem itself is an experience, that words can have a real, physical effect on people. As Rilke put it, 'song is existence', where poetry is life itself, and making poetry is not a commentary 'about' life, but is life itself. This feeling about poetry recalls the *alchuringa* mythic dreamtime of the Australian aborigines, where the world is sung into existence (a notion also found in Western occultism, in God's cosmic song, in the 'music of the spheres').[6] As Peter Redgrove says, 'the purpose of art is to inspire us with our own creative energies' (SS). That is, art makes life, gives life.

RIMBAUD. For a time, when he was 16 or so, until he was 19, art was crucial for the psychic well-being of the ever-restless Arthur Rimbaud, another of Peter Redgrove's inspirations. Rimbaud was the amazing poet who escaped from the utterly bland provincial town of Charleville in Northern France to wander the streets of Paris in near-poverty (and later London, Europe and Africa). After writing his *Illuminations* and *A Season in Hell*, the most extraordinary poems of French – and world – literature, Rimbaud renounced it all for what appeared to have been a hellish and profoundly boring life in Aden and Africa.

Arthur Rimbaud is the tornado of world poetry. He outblasts just about every other poet. For Redgrove, Rimbaud became his spiritual guide, his Virgil: 'Rimbaud escorted me many times through Hell and back again', wrote Redgrove for the centenary celebrations of Rimbaud's death (Rim, 172). Rimbaud – and Redgrove – is, like Orpheus, always descending into hell and returning, a continuous journey of Out and Back, In and Back, Down and Back. This is the basic spiritual journey of the shaman, the fragmentation and rebirth of the self. Redgrove is constantly rebirthing himself, as the artist does, in each work. For Redgrove, lovemaking could be a way of travelling to the other world of death, as a shaman does, as well as the supersensual realm: 'coitus consists of two people hurling themselves into death but with the ability to return, to live and to remember', he wrote in 'The Duct' (CM, 107).

This Descent and Return is a central experience in Peter Redgrove's world. He links it with Isis, Orpheus and Jesus, with the Black Goddess, with the 'underlife' of John Cowper Powys, and with the break-up and reconstitution of the menstrual cycle. More of this later.

The two things – the synæsthetic experience and the prose poem, one of Rimbaud's innovations which Redgrove took up in his later work (in his *Alchemical Journal*) – go hand in hand in Redgrove's art as in Rimbaud's art. In a similar fashion, those long, flowing stanzas of Rilke's *Duino Elegies* were an integral part of that revelation which came upon Rilke so suddenly – in the form of the 'terrifying Angel'.

SEX–MAGIC–POETRY–CORNWALL

2.2 Poetry and Life: The Strangeness of Strangeness

Peter Redgrove's poetic code is to create poems which describe or actualize the strangeness of living. The strangeness is here, all around people, he says, but they become immune to it. The poet's task is therefore to refresh body and soul, so that the incredible beauty and strangeness of life is once again experienced. The emphasis is on direct experience, not on abstraction or distance. Redgrove's poetic ethic is one of direct touches – the Blakean (and Coleridgean) direct contact stemming from the cleansing of the senses. One thinks too of D.H. Lawrence's touch of tenderness, the pure touch, which reactivates hidden/ latent/ unconscious feelings, or Rainer Maria Rilke's apprehension of the invisible, or Arthur Rimbaud's alchemy of the word. It is this touch, this new relation, that counts, that reactivates livingness. As Lawrence said: '[b]lossoming means the establishing of a pure, *new* relationship with all the cosmos. This is the state of heaven.'[1]

Peter Redgrove's life-philosophy of poetic awakening was expressed in one of my favourites of his statements, which he wrote in a letter to me of 1993:

> …this 'strangeness' is 'strange' because reality is so fucking extraordinary, and strange too because most of us try to live without strangeness, and construct something called the 'ordinary' which never existed. Actually, the strangeness is so ordinary as to be quite natural. The strangeness is wonder and what is wondered at is so wonderful that it is strange we do not wonder more.[2]

All the wonder of living is all around us. It always was, it always is, it always will be. There is nowhere else Paradise could possibly be. Many mystics have said this – Meister Eckhart, Hui-Neng, Chuang-tzu. Come on, *wake up*, the mystics say. 'Leap into the boundless and make it your home,' said the great Chinese philosopher Chuang-tzu, perfectly describing the artistic act of creation.[3] We are dead, so we must wake up. This is the basic philosophy of any number of artists – André Gide, John Cowper Powys, Anaïs Nin and Arthur Rimbaud. And Redgrove too. In *Alchemy For Women*, Redgrove wrote:

> Actuality and dream interact. No reality can remain 'ordinary' if it illuminated by its dream. No dream can remain fantasy while grounded in actuality. Actuality is the spirit of the dream; dream is actuality's soul. Both dream and actuality are real. (27-28)

Take Redgrove's poem 'A World', which is, like 'Shadow-Silk', one of those passionate and bewildering pieces that's about anything and everything. Like 'Shadow-Silk', 'A World' overflows with life. In Redgrove's poesie, everything is swirled up together. In 'A World', the lines race from sugar and rain through convolvulus, perfume, snails, wood, clocks, roses, pine-cones, honey, balsam, forests, eyes, etc. The effect is vertiginous and vortiginous, a veritable vortex of words whirled up by the poet's shamanic incantations. What does it 'mean'? It 'means' everything, it points towards everything, it 'opens' the reader out to everything (its 'meaning' is precisely in its experience, in the poem as experience).

The poem, like the best of Redgrove's (or anybody's) poems, opens things out. It expands awareness and experience. It is profoundly *interested* in the world. It is a poem that loves the world. In loving the world, the poem sets out to *create a world of its own*. The poem thus becomes a space of its own, the 'magic ring' of Robert Graves, that poetic space that Redgrove calls the 'womb-place', or *temenos*, or creative laboratory, or Merlin's *esplumeor*.

The world is amazing, so the poet sets out to create something that reflects this amazement – her/ his amazement at being in the world, the amazement that arises from her/ his *relationship* with the world (if being alive isn't amazing, what is?). The poem is the poet's reflection of the amazing nature of the world. But, as Redgrove argues, the poem itself can be astonishing, just as astonishing as the world. The poem is thus not a mirror reflecting the experience of tradition, but is an *experience in itself*. The poem becomes part of the world – part of the amazing nature of the world.

SEX–MAGIC–POETRY–CORNWALL

Take 'Grimmanderson on Tresco', Redgrove's amazing meltdown of fairy tales, mythic imagery, eroticism, landscape, beasts, Christianity and biology, all whirled up together by the force of the poet's sense of being alive. ('Grimmanderson' refers of course to Jacob and Wilhelm Grimm and Hans Christian Andersen – there's plenty of fairy and folk tale imagery and motifs in Redgrove's poetry, as well science fiction and fantasy. Redgrove regarded Grimms' collection of fairy tales as 'a kind of *Bible* of the Goddess, a book of epiphanies' [WW. 122]).

Life itself is amazing, this is the point. Life doesn't need way-out fantasies, violent religions and or distant but merciless deities to make it astonishing. As Rilke said, 'existence is magical'.[4] And Redgrove was fond of saying that 'real life is romantic and ghostly' (quoting G.W. Pabst, the German film director).[5]

Joseph Campbell wrote that '[p]oets are simply those who have made a profession and a lifestyle of being in touch with their bliss' (118). For Campbell, life can – and should – be blissful. That is, one must get into the right relation with life, with the world. He calls it 'following your bliss'. In bliss, the epiphany or radiance shines through, and life becomes full of light.

Peter Redgrove spoke of similar experiences. For him, ecstasy usually comes from relaxation exercises, or the yoga of walking, or, often, lovemaking. After lovemaking, reality 'shines', as the mystics might put it. Redgrove spoke of the 'light of the body'. Mystics have their own terms for such experiences – there is the Zen Buddhist *satori* or enlightenment, the Hindu *samadhi*, the Catholic *unio mystica* or spiritual marriage, while James Joyce coined 'epiphany' for the true æsthetic experience.

Rainer Maria Rilke wrote in his *Duino Elegies* of the need to make reality transparent, instead of opaque: the goal is to live in 'the Open'. As Rilke explained in a letter:

> In that supreme "open" World, all *exist* – one cannot say "simultaneously", for it is precisely the discontinuation of time which determines their existence. The past plunges everywhere into a deep

SEX–MAGIC–POETRY–CORNWALL

Being.[6]

To render life 'open' is the goal (open to the invisible realms, beyond the veil of 'ordinary' life, using what Redgrove called the 'dark' senses). Redgrove continually emphasized the importance of producing visionary states – the states of post-coital bliss, of daydreaming, of meditation, of sleep, of poetic trance, and so on. These states are usually relegated to the sidelines of society, but they are not only crucial, claims Redgrove, they are normal. They are the very stuff of life. So Redgrove remarked:

> Don't daydream, Johnny! Well, of course, daydreaming is exactly what I have to teach my art students. I have to teach them yoga-nidra, which is daydreaming. To develop it into responsible fantasy. (SS)

Redgrove brought these trance or altered states that are usually ignored into the foreground. He normalizes the seemingly abnormal. States of consciousness the establishment regards with suspicion as 'strange', 'perverse' or 'wrong', are for Redgrove completely ordinary. But also extraordinary. And useful. These experiences of the 'dark senses' are not imaginary but real. Redgrove writes: '[m]y point is that what one envisions are actualities which play upon our unconscious senses.'[7]

So the daydream, the artistic trance, the post-coital reverie, is put to good use in Redgrove's poetics. He advocated, rightly, the creative use of these states which everyone experiences everyday. He recommended keeping a dream diary, for instance, so that dreams are integrated into everyday life, instead of being ignored. (The diary or journal or workbook was central to Redgrove's working practice).

SEX–MAGIC–POETRY–CORNWALL

2.3   Shamanism

The basis for this poetic experimentation or mode of living is shamanism. The figure of the archaic shaman is the origin of the artist/ poet/ magician/ visionary. The shaman is the daydreamer, the angelic traveller to other worlds, the godmaker, the witch, the medicine man and witch doctor, the 'scientist of the strange', the original magician. As Mircea Eliade writes in his classic work on shamanism:

> As to Orpheus, his myth displays several elements that can be compared to the shamanic ideology and technique. The most significant is, of course, his descent to Hades to bring back the soul of his wife, Eurydice... Orpheus displays other characteristics of a "Great Shaman": his healing art, his love for music and animals, his "charms", his power of divination. Even his character of "culture hero" is not contradiction to the best shamanic tradition – was not the 'first shaman" the messenger sent by God to defend humanity against diseases and to civilize it? A final detail of the Orpheus myth is clearly shamanic. Cut off by the bacchantes and thrown into the Gebrus, Orpheus' head floated to Lesbos, singing. It later served as an oracle... (391)

Redgrove is one of these shamanic, Orphic, Dionysian, Pentecostal, fierily lyrical poets (one thinks of poets such as Sappho, William Shakespeare, Arthur Rimbaud and Friedrich Hölderlin). Shamanism features in much of Redgrove's poetry (though it is not always obvious). The shaman can travel to other worlds; the poet does exactly the same thing. The invisible worlds in religion are utterly 'other' – Heaven is at the top of the World Tree, for instance. For Redgrove, however, the strange, invisible worlds are right here, all around. So the poet descends into life itself, by descending into her/ himself first. In shamanism, there is a deep identification between inner and outer, between private and public, between all realms of experience. This is also the key concept of Western magic, the 'as above, so below' of hermeticism.

The shaman is the 'maker', and the Greek *poeitas*, the word for 'poet', means 'maker'. The shaman, like the poet, dreams society's dreams. The shaman is the 'technician of ecstasy', to use Eliade's useful term (1972, 1). Robert Graves spoke of the 'poetic trance', that shamanic state in which the poet creates.[1] For Graves, authentic poems came out of this state – other sorts of 'waking' poems were not the real thing (i.e., poetic authenticity meant poetry composed in a trance). The Goddess or Muse, for Graves, presides over this poetic trance. Every shaman has a different god – indeed, the shaman is her/ his own god.[2] Here's Eliade again:

> Poetic creation still remains an act of perfect spiritual freedom. Poetry remakes and the prolongs language; every poetic language begins by being a secret language, that is, the creation of a personal universe, of a completely closed world. The purest poetic act seems to recreate language from an inner experience that, like the ecstasy or the religious inspiration of "primitives", reveals the essence of things. (510)

The feminine realm lies behind much of shamanism. Take Shakespeare's major shaman in the plays, Prospero: his magic comes from the witch Sycorax. The shaman, like Jesus or Orpheus, descends into hell, and Hades is of course a feminine realm in Western religion (there is the Mouth of Hell, which is the vagina/ womb, a connection made explicit in much of Western art – in *Troilus and Cressida* or *Romeo and Juliet*, for example). In Redgrove's poetry, too, the male creator takes his energy from the woman/ Goddess: he goes down to her soul-space using the 'dark' senses and brings back his visions.

Arthur Rimbaud is the great shamanic poet of modern times. The shamanic possession took hold of him and wrestled with him very powerfully. Shamanic possession can be seen as insanity, and of course, as Shakespeare noted in *Love's Labour's Lost*, the poet, the lover, the fool and the madman are closely linked. In psychological terms, one can't easily distinguish between the artist, the genius, the psychotic and the criminal – they share states of obsession and extremity.

Rimbaud announced, in his famous 'lettre du voyant' of May, 1871, when he 16, that the poet must become a 'seer'.[3] He then proceeded to show the world just how astonishing shamanic or 'seer' poetry can be. Any number of Peter Redgrove's poems can be seen as shamanic. (The best of Redgrove's poetry can be placed along side Rimbaud's poems, though I don't think Redgrove himself would rate himself on the same level as Rimbaud).

Take Peter Redgrove's wonderful 'Rainmaking Exercise': a man goes into a wood (a shamanic place, relating to the Cosmic Tree, to sacred groves, to Eleusis of Greek mythology, to Dante's *selva oscura*, to Druids, etc). The images of electricity in this piece, for instance, are purely shamanic, for one of the shaman's magical abilities is to be able to conjure and control fire. The conjuring up of the storm, thunder and lightning in Redgrove's poems echoes the acts of magicians and shamans everywhere (one recalls, again, Prospero and Ariel whipping up the storm in the opening of *The Tempest*, while witches during Shakespeare's time, as in any other time, could create storms.)

2.4   The Colours of Alchemy

The language of Peter Redgrove's 'Rainmaking Exercise' poem is shamanic ('witchy', 'wildman', 'magical', etc), and the colours are those of alchemy: black, white and gold. Arthur Rimbaud created his notion of the 'alchemy of the word' ('J'inventerai la couleur des voyelles!'), where poetry becomes alchemy, a magical transformative process which can create the Philosopher's Stone out of the stuff of life. (The Philosopher's Stone is a loaded and somewhat misleading term, like the Holy Grail. So Redgrove spoke in terms of the 'Great Work' of alchemy, or searching for the elixir, rather than the Philosopher's Stone.).

Redgrove's poetry is shot through with alchemy and alchemical allusions (see 'The Alchemical Honeymoon', for example, or the extracts from *The Alchemical Journal*). Look at the colours of Redgrove's poems, those blacks, whites and reds which he keeps returning to time and again. These are the colours of alchemy, and of life.[1] Redgrove is obsessed in particular with black and white. He is always describing white shirts – how he loves white shirts!

> I love white sleeves
> The warm arms in them
> Are like warm sunlight in water
> (from 'One Half of Three Poems Twice' [Ark, 236])

There's a white shirt in 'Rainmaking Exercise', for example. Look at any of Redgrove's poems and you'll find a plethora of black and white imagery, a mythology of *yin-yang* transformations, the one always transmuting into the other.

White is skin, clothes, lightning, the Moon, clouds, water and glass in Redgrove's poetry. Black is the Black Goddess, the unknown/ invisible/ strange/ night/ unconscious/ sixth or 'dark' sense. Red is the colour of life in full bloom – blood, passion, emotion, anger, sun, honey, etc. Redgrove constantly spins these three colours together. The reader's always aware of white lightning in black skies. Or golden honey – in 'The Case' (one of Redgrove's first really grand poems), one hears of '[b]lood, cider, rainbow, and the apples still warm after sunset' (SP, 50). That line contains six references to warm or red things. The first part of 'The Comforter' (a poem that nearly made it into this collection), is a lightning strike of hot/ red/ orange/ honey-warm things:

> The spectrum of all honeys, the sweet rainbow:
> White clover; green honey
> Of sycamore and limetree; acacia of pale gold
>
> And brilliant sun-honey of dandelion; almost black
> Gathered from chestnut and buckwheat;
> The fetid honey of the laurel

SEX–MAGIC–POETRY–CORNWALL

Of privet and ragwort too, though to the bees
It is excellent, they help themselves freely;
And the thyme and rosemary are ever-thick with bees. (AB, 95)

Red relates to the blood mysteries of the feminine in Redgrove's multiverse, which is life itself at its deepest level (Redgrove called menstrual blood 'magic blood' or 'wise blood'). Honey, beer, apples, bees, flowers – these red-tinted and golden-hued images are Redgrove specialities. (The apple, for instance, Redgrove, was 'an emblem of woman's nature', 'her magic', 'her witch-nature'. It was linked with the magic number five, the pentagram, the five-pointed star. Inevitably, Redgrove reworked the famous scene in the Garden of Eden with Adam and Eve and the apple, giving it a feminist, menstrual slant in *The Wise Wound* [137f]).

Black and white together clearly define the twin poles of life, the eternal dualities of Western religion, from ancient Zorasterian/Manicheanism onwards through Christianity to Renaissance alchemy and modern Jungian psychology. In alchemy, of course, black and white refer to particular processes, stages in the transmutation of the elements on the journey towards making the Philosopher's Stone, the Great Work of alchemists.

All these things melt into one in Peter Redgrove's multiverse: poetry-alchemy-shamanism-Chinese sex magic-Indian yoga-love-poetry. They are all connected, and the poetic experience links them all together. Redgrove's is a unified worldview, a mythopœia which always tries to unite the multifarious experiences of living.

SEX–MAGIC–POETRY–CORNWALL

2.5   Deschooling of the Senses

The super-gorgeous Arthur Rimbaud, aged 16 (only 16!), wrote: 'the Poet makes himself a seer by a long and gigantic derangement of all the senses. All forms of love, suffering and madness.'[1] Mr Redgrove, among others, notes that Rimbaud says a 'rational' derangement of the senses (Redgrove prefers to say 'deschooling'), meaning a systematic and scientific de-schooling, in the manner of the scientific approaches of the so-called 'Naturalist' novelists, such as Emile Zola and Gustave Flaubert. Rimbaud's experiment with himself, then, was a rigorous one, not just a wild dive into decadence and debauchery (although Rimbaud enjoyed plenty of that too).

Arthur Rimbaud's technique was synæsthesia. That is, the multi-sensory intoxication of poetry, a poetry 'containing everything, smells, sounds, colours' (309). Rimbaud called it an 'alchemy of the word' and, in his extraordinary *A Season in Hell*, he wrote:

> I like idiot paintings, over doors, stage sets, backcloths for acrobats, signs, popular prints, old-fashioned literature, church latin, erotic books with misspellings, novels of our grandmothers, fairy tales, little children's books, old operas, foolish refrains, naïve rhythms.
> (from *Delirium II: Alchemy of the Word*, my translation)

The Rimbaud-poet was so hungry for life. He had such a lust for life. He wanted to swallow everything. All at once, whole. Redgrove has a similar appetite. Nothing is too big for his poesie to absorb. Sometimes Redgrove is even more ecstatic than Rimbaud – amazing, but true. In his poems, you'll see ecstasies to rival those of Rimbaud or Rilke. Most of the ecstasies of Redgrove's concern lovemaking, women or the natural world.

At times, Redgrove is more Rimbaudian than Rimbaud himself. Take this stanza from 'The Laundromat as Prayer-Wheel':

SEX–MAGIC–POETRY–CORNWALL

It is the night of the Mystery of White Shapes,
The angel is here, a splendid presence, like electricity in linen,
I fold the double sheet up, I wrestle with its wings. (AB, 59)

This is very shamanic, alchemical and Rimbaudian: the angel, for instance, is supremely the shaman in full achievement, or the angel is the Philosopher's Stone or hermaphrodite (or magical child) of alchemy, the transcendent union of male/ female, black/ white, sun/ moon (see *The Alchemical Journal* extracts here). In Rimbaud's *œuvre*, the angel is the 'genie' in that most potent poem of his *Illuminations* ('Genie'). In Redgrove's stanza there is also shamanic fire (electricity), the Rimbaudian commonplace (linen), Gnostic duality (black/ white imagery), Promethean struggle (wrestling with the wings) and alchemical incubation (night as the womb-space for rebirth).

And this is going on all the time in Redgrove's verse. Look at his poems: you'll see many images of rebirth, of alchemical transmutation, of shamanic fire, of magical trance. It all seems so extraordinary, but that's Redgrove's main point. It ain't extraordinary at all. Not really. All this intense but blissful feeling is quite 'ordinary' *and* extraordinary. It occurs everyday. All you have to do is to come alive, get into the I-Thou relation, as Martin Buber would put it, or the I-It relation of Georg Groddeck, or get quick with 'Faculty X', as Colin Wilson might say, or 'follow your bliss', as Joseph Campbell said, or come into being, as D.H. Lawrence would say ('[t]o be alive, to be man alive, to be the whole man alive: that is the point' Lawrence wrote),[2] or become a 'seer', as Rimbaud says, or achieve 'deep Being' or Buddhahood, as Rilke might say (see his 'Buddha in Glory'), or sink into your 'mythology' or 'life-illusion' as old John Cowper Powys used to say.

SEX–MAGIC–POETRY–CORNWALL

2.6   Synæsthesia

The aim, then, of Peter Redgrove's poetry, is to turn life into alchemical gold, to make every potential moment blissful. The method is poetic synæsthesia. Redgrove cited George Whalley, who says that synæsthesia is 'almost a definition of poetry' (PR, 9). So, for Redgrove, Rimbaudian synæsthesia means 'the joining together of all the senses and their mutual illumination thereby' (PR,10). (And when he means all of the senses, he means the five that combine to produce the supernatural sixth sense; or maybe the sixth sense is the positive mixture of the five 'rational' senses.)

Consequently, Redgrove is a poet who is 'visionary' in all of the senses. He constantly focuses on smell, for instance, or touch, rather than sight. There's no poet I can think of with such an acutely developed mythology of scent. Redgrove devotes a section of his major poetic treatise, *The Black Goddess and the Sixth Sense*, to scent, to 'extra-sensuous perception'. 'Odour is scenery, scenery is smell', he writes in the poem 'Fly Buddha' (Mud, 21), and in 'Instead of Ghosts' he describes a '[s]ouk | Of perfumes' (Tarot, 13). In 'Superstition' he says that 'the other world comes through with a certain note | Which may be a perfume' WNP, 98). The 'cunny smell' in the poem 'Rescue' that comes off the May trees is no illusion: rather, it is 'the fourth dimension | Of perfume making all the more real' (OE, 10).

In his poems, scent plays a major role: it is difficult to overstress its importance. There is, for instance, the wonderful perfume of menstruation in the poem 'Starlight', and many other examples. (And scents are described by the Redgrove-poet in terms of other senses: the *colour*, or the *feel* of a smell, for instance. Scents are one of the 'invisible' experiences which the Redgrove-poet makes visible in his poetry.)

SEX–MAGIC–POETRY–CORNWALL

2.7 The Language of Ecstasy

A new language is needed, as Arthur Rimbaud knew, for this new synæsthetic poetry. One sees Peter Redgrove stretching for a new vocabulary of scent – in the phrase 'bed-opiums', in the poem 'Starlight', for example, which is so apt, and everyone has smelt them. But the language of smell is poorly developed. Our visual sense, as Marshall McLuhan, Slavoj Zizek, Paul Virillo and many others have noted, is well-developed. Hence Redgrove has to employ visual descriptions and metaphors to depict, or hint at, odours, touches and tastes. So he talks about 'the light of the body' for that glowing feeling after orgasm. Or he transfers scents into visions, or touches into visual imagery. You have to do this if you can't find the right words to describe something. So in the poem 'Blackthorn Winter', Redgrove writes: '[t]o smell the touch of the wind, to hear the contours' (UR, 4).

Peter Redgrove's poetry is a mythopœia of ecstasies, but ecstasies which must be integrated into everyday life. The first great ecstatic poem in Redgrove's *œuvre* is probably 'The Case' (1966). It contains the Redgrovean ecstasy full of heavily sensual experiences, couched in the three alchemical colours of life:

> And I swam in the thunderstorm in the river of blood, oil and cider,
> And I saw the blue of my recovery open around me in the water
> Blood, cider, rainbow, and the apples still warm after sunset
> Dashed in the cold downpour, and so this mother-world
> Opened around me and I lay in the perfumes after rain out of the
>   river
> Tugging the wet grass, eyes squeezed, straining to the glory,
> The burst of white glory like the whitest cloud rising to the sun.
> …It was the mother-world wet with perfume. It was something about
>   God. (SP,50)

POWYS. Among British novelists, it is John Cowper Powys who has captured most accurately the synæsthetic experiences of life, where so many tiny and seemingly inconsequential sensations fuse into illumination. Powys's *Autobiography* (1934) is one long record of ecstasies and sensations. Redgrove liked to quote Powys from his *Autobiography* (from page 168): Powys has been out walking and is returning to Cambridge with his walking stick:

> What I am revealing to you now is the deepest and most essential secret of my life. My thoughts were lost in my sensations; and my sensations were of a kind so difficult to describe that I could write a volume upon them and still not really have put them down. But the field-dung upon my boots, the ditch-mud plastered thick, with little bits of dead grass in it, against the turned-up ends of my trousers, the feel of my oak-stick "Sacred" whose every indentation and corrugation and curve I knew as well as those on my hand, the salty taste of half-dried sweat upon my lips, the delicious swollenness of my fingers, the sullen sweet weariness of my legs, the indescribable happiness of my calm, dazed, lulled, wind-drugged, air-drunk spirit, were all, after their kind, a sort of thinking, though of *exactly what*, it would be very hard for me to explain.[1]

You don't get this all-round, multi-sensory description of being alive so often in the works of Dante Alighieri, Homer, Lev Tolstoy or Miguel Cervantes. It is such an accurate description of walking (a favourite Powys activity). Yet, as Powys says, it doesn't add up to much – he can't say what it all 'means'. That's why such experiences are ignored. Yet they are central to living. This is what Redgrove reactivates in his poesie, these sensations which form 'the deepest and most essential secret of... life', as Powys says. (They don't have to 'mean' anything: *they are*. They are experiences, perhaps beyond meaning. Asking what they 'mean' is the wrong question. What do they *feel* like? is better).

John Cowper Powys was an ecstatic writer, who worked best when he was moving from one ecstasy to another. It is the same with Peter Redgrove. H. W. Fawkner remarked that Powys was not a 'stream of consciousness' writer, in the manner of James Joyce or Virginia Woolf; rather, he was a 'stream-of-ecstasy' writer.[2] Redgrove admired Fawkner's book on John Cowper Powys, and we discussed it when were talking about Powys. Fawkner wrote: '[e]verything signifies. The world becomes text, and the reading of that ecstasy... Exterior reality becomes ecstatic reality' (ib., 152-4). This recalls Redgrove's tenet that '[a]ll surfaces become depths', and that all of life can be blissful, if one becomes opened in the right fashion. Powys wrote in his *In Defence of Sensuality*: '[w]hat this psychic sensuous ecstasy that I am defending really implies is a *direct embrace of life*'.[3]

John Cowper Powys and Peter Redgrove are right. But in the hustle and bustle of so-called 'modern' living, these sensations get smothered by all kinds of other, seemingly 'important' information. Yet, interestingly, Redgrove said that '[a]ll surfaces become depths.'[4] What he meant is that all those things you thought were irrelevant and superficial are in fact very relevant and deep. The other superficial things – television, say, or money – are dropped in favour of multi-sensory sensualism. Redgrove explained further:

> There is a point in sex when you arrive at a different level which is more solid, real and strange than what you were accustomed to. Language can record this... and can induct author and reader back into that state – it leaves the doors open, the surfaces deep.[5]

Redgrove is discussing sex here, but he could be talking about the whole poetic experience. Poetry renders reality 'deep' and 'open', as lovemaking does. The poetic trance is identical with the orgasmic trance. The idea is to make the orgasmic state, and the dream state, as creative as the poetic state of trance. All trances interconnect – become one. The point, Redgrove often said (quoting Frank Avray Wilson at least twice in *Alchemy For Women*), was not to interpret dreams in terms of ordinary life, but to interpret reality in terms of dreams.

This poetic sensualism manifests itself throughout Redgrove's poetry, but it attains its deepest intensity with collections such as *The Apple-Broadcast* (1981), *The Man Named East* (1985) and the later books: *In the Hall of the Saurians, The First Earthquake* and *Under the Reservoir*.

SEX–MAGIC–POETRY–CORNWALL

From *In the Country of the Skin* and *Dr Faust's Sea-Spiral Spirit* (1972-73) onwards, Peter Redgrove's poetry became fully synæsthetic: this breakthrough was bound up with Penelope Shuttle's problems with menstruation and the dreams of this time (see "How We Met"). The dreams fed both Shuttle's and Redgrove's work, and led to *The Wise Wound: Menstruation and Everywoman* (1978) and the follow-up, *Alchemy For Women* (1995).

Two poems from *Dr Faust's Sea-Spiral Spirit* demonstrate as well as any the Rimbaudian sensualism at the heart of Redgrove's mythopœia: 'Shadow-Silk' and 'The Moon Disposes'. 'Shadow-Silk' is an archetypical Redgrove piece, with its fiercely black-and-white imagery, its description of floods and being drenched, its non-stop flow of lines, its incessant rhythm and its urge towards strangeness-in-the-ordinary:

> We are heels over ears in love.
> The window-frame blackens.
> Below, the trees flood darkly,
> The wind butts in the curtain
> A doddering forehead.
> We have a one candle.
> Your hair is like a weir,
> Or fields of posture,
> In terrace upon terrace
> Rising forest murmur,
> And across the garden
> Frothily flows the ghost. (Dr, 5)

And from 'The Moon Disposes':

> Hours late we walk among the strewn dead
> Of this tide's sacrifice. There are strangled mussels:
> The moon pulls back the lid, the wind unhinges them,
> They choke on fans, they are bunched blue, black band.
> The dead are beautiful, and give us life.
> The setting wave recoils
> In flocculence of blood-in-crystal,
> It is medusa parched to hoofprints, broken bands,
> Which are beautiful, and give us life. (Dr, 7)

SEX–MAGIC–POETRY–CORNWALL

After all, Redgrove doesn't describe weird, perverse occurrences. Everything in his poetry is easily approachable. His vocabulary, for example, is very simple, refreshingly simple: nothing difficult or arcane here, in his use of words such as *black, flood, shadow, tree, flower, cloud*. He employs simple stanzaic forms – the three-line/ *terza rima* stanza is a favourite (as with Sylvia Plath and Dante Alighieri).

Redgrove was great with titles: his titles are instantly recognizable as Redgrovean, like his lines, images, themes and landscapes. These are some poem titles taken from one book, 1981's *The Apple Broadcast*: 'Cloud-Rustling', 'In the Glass House', 'Grimmanderson On Tresco', 'Using the Dark', 'Orchard With Wasps', 'The White, Night-Flying Moths Called 'Souls'', 'Pheromones', and 'Wet Angel'. Those could only be poems by Peter Redgrove.

Peter Redgrove uses hyphenated terms often, as in the title 'Shadow-Silk', or in the poem 'Frankenstein in the Forest', where he writes of 'Man-skin' (SP, 78), or of 'cursing-lipstick', in 'Four Tall Tales' (*The Weddings at Nether Powers*, 123), or 'she was well-clitorised' (i.e., enjoyed many orgasms) in 'The Dark Bell' (FVC, 62). He has to use hyphenations, because he is constantly searching for the right expression language. Anaïs Nin often used words hyphenated together, moaning that there was no language of sex. It had to be invented, she said, so she had a go. One of my favourite of Redgrove's coinings terms is in the last line of 'Under the Duvet': '[b]irthwet from its egg of the newborn angel (SP, 189).

'Birthwet' neatly sums up the slippery nature of birth, for birth is all wetness – all that water and blood, as the womb becomes the world, and the Inside becomes all Outside, where inner womb-space becomes all outer world-space, and a baby is born. The world becomes a 'yoni-verse', as Redgrove calls it in 'The Yoniversity at Rock' (from *My Father's Trapdoors*).

In 'Name of Rock of Shells', Redgrove writes:

> I genuflect
> To the moonlit pond, I am running the sound

SEX–MAGIC–POETRY–CORNWALL

>   Of the rain backwards and getting a fast tape
>   Full of voices crying plashy names abruptly
>   Enumerating the dead and new born...
>   (WNP, 129)

Peter Redgrove is always doing this in his poetry, running natural sounds backwards to form a new sound, full of voices (there's so much emphasis on sound, breathing, wind and air in Redgrove's work, one wonders if he might've been an experimental musician in another life, like, say, Brian Eno).

The birth experience is central to Redgrove's mythopœia – in his poem 'Delivery Hymn' for instance, where the Christ-child is 'warm-shirted in membrane' (SP, 149). So many poems are drenched in the Redgroverse, the Redgrove multiverse. Take this section of 'Living in Falmouth', which is a long poem, much as all of Redgrove's poetry is one long poem. Every line contains a watery reference:

>   Orion with his brilliant cock shining like the wet spiderweb,
>   Like a ladder of light heavier than all the world,
>   Climbing in his drenched plumage like pulsing snow,
>   Like a silver beaten so long that it gives back light in pulsing
>   juice,
>   Or like a rainfall so massive it gluts and cannot fall,
>   Or like a full-rigged black ship, sailing with all knots white,
>   Or like wet herringbones at the rim of a great black plate...
>   (SP, 132)

The tendency to gush is common in mystics and mystical poets. They are so charged up with energy and experiences, and they have to let it all flood out. So they over-write. They write and write. One sees this clearly in writers such as D.H. Lawrence, who gushed madly, or William Wordsworth, in his *Prelude*, or in William Shakespeare's plays, in John Cowper Powys's novels (Powys's *A Glastonbury Romance* is one of the biggest floods in the English language, and, rightly enough, Powys's extravaganza winds up with a gigantic flood that engulfs the New Jerusalem of Albion and leaves everyone seeking sanctuary up on

Glastonbury Tor).

So in Redgrove's work, there is a tendency to gush, to pour, to flood. The sexual connations of flooding ain't lost on him. There is the flood of water at birth, before labour begins, for instance. 'I love getting wet', announces the poet in Redgrove's novel *The Beekeepers* (16). Redgrove himself lived in Falmouth, surrounded by water – not just the ocean, but also the Carrick Roads estuary system – and this Cornish seascape feeds all of his poesie. 'Water is my element, the feminine element. Yes, so I think it's urethral contrasted with phallic,' he says (MR). Rivers are as prominent as the ocean in Redgrove's poetry; there are poems about the River Thames, for instance (and Falmouth nestles between a river and the sea).

Peter Redgrove is the only poet I know of who has written a poem describing the inner workings of a fountain. A traditional emblem, a fountain, found in Francesco Petrarch's eulogies to his beloved Vaucluse landscape, and in many mediæval illuminated manuscripts and images of enclosed gardens (relating to the Virgin Mary, a symbol of the feminine, purity, plenitude, and so on). But in Redgrove's poetry, it is the plumbing that fascinates him. One of his collections of poems, *The Working of Water* (1984), is devoted to the mythology of water and waterworks, reservoirs, flow, dowsing, etc.

Redgrove literally drenches his poetry with water. Any number of Redgrove's poems take water as the main subject, from the homages to pubs and drinking ('Legible Hours', 'Alchemical Buveur', 'Buveur's Farewell'), to the poems about bodies and water ('The Moisture-Number', 'Wet Sportswomen', 'Wet Pinup', 'A Dewy Garment'), to fish and aquaria ('Three Aquarium Portraits'), to wells ('Ancient Well'), to hoses and sprinklers ('Lawn Sprinkler and Lighthouse'), to the poems about water on a grand scale, either in the sky, in clouds and stars, or under the ground ('Under the Reservoir', 'Water-Table'), or in lakes, reservoirs, fountains, rivers and oceans ('Waterworks as Spiritual Powerhouse', 'Rain on Vaux Hill', 'Lake Now-and-Again'). Was it John Milton or Henry Miller who said they love everything that flows. Or was it Heraclitus?

What happens, technically, is a tendency in Peter Redgrove's poetry towards prose. Some critics (such as (Stella Stocker) dislike the prose-like nature of any poetry, and of Redgrove's poetry. Arthur Rimbaud would gush, and often, like Emily Dickinson, employed the dash – to connect different streams – of experience – which were coming at him – so fast – because of his mystical ecstasies – so the dash allows for the kind of flow appropriate for mysticism. Rimbaud also went for the prose poem, which also enabled opening out in all directions. Then there is John Cowper Powys, the master of the long sentence, or *longueur*, as G. Wilson Knight called it.[6] Some of Powys's sentences famously ran on for whole paragraphs, with plenty of sub-clauses and diversions.

Peter Redgrove's poetic technique stems from his method of making poems. He first of all wrote in notebooks. He collected notes, snippets, observations, experiences, from all manner of sources. He caught lots of live things, like children catch newts in jars, and kept them in a journal. These were then woven into 'second-stage' 'imagery' notebooks. Then came a prose draft for each poem, then an all-important incubation period (as with the sealed writing), and so on, and on, refining, moving the poems about, changing their form from prose to poetry, until, as in alchemy, some final transformation is hopefully accomplished (see "Work and Incubation").

Sometimes the same research material can wind up in different poems. Have a look at No. 17 from *In the Esplumeor*, for instance, a prose poem, which crops up again in 'Indications' (this time as *terza rima* poetry). And sometimes in Redgrove's novels: the prose poem 'Dance the Putrefact' appears in the novel *The Facilitators* (119).

In Peter Redgrove's *œuvre* as in John Cowper Powys's there is a love of the long sentence, carried on over many stanzas, very long lines, lines that, as in Walt Whitman's verse, run on and on. So that everything in the poem is chained together, and occurs in a continuous present moment, linked by a continuous sense of rhythm and space, an

SEX–MAGIC–POETRY–CORNWALL

Eternal Now of a single weaving sentence. With no full or stops there are no breaks (a common technique in modern poetry is to dispense with punctuation): the experience of the poem is unified. There are many sensations or insights in the poems, but, due to the single-sentence structure, they are all melted together. They coalesce in synæsthesia.

The poem 'Round Pylons', in *The First Earthquake*, is six three-line stanzas in one sentence (FE, 36), while large sections of Redgrove's poems are single sentences ('Grimmanderson on Tresco', 'Pheromones', 'Rainmaking Exercise' and 'Four Poems of Love and Transition'). In a late poem like 'Purity', five stanzas are composed of one sentence. Rarely did Redgrove use the pentameter, the blank verse of William Shakespeare, or the rugged Anglo-Saxon half-line. In later pieces, Redgrove employed the prose poem – most successfully in *In the Esplumeor: An Alchemical Journal*.

Redgrove did employ strong rhythms, like Ted Hughes, like most mystical utterers. Look at the outpourings of St Teresa, St Bernard or Jal-al al-Din Rumi, and one'll see phrases repeated, slightly altered, but poured forth rhythmically. Redgrove used rhythm as the shaman uses her/ his drum to beat up ecstasy, just as the poet-smith in the forge of alchemical creativity hammers out art on the anvil.[7]

The strong sense of rhythm meant the lengthy lines of Redgrove's poetry didn't become mere prose broken up into stanzas. The notebooks might have been written in prose, but by the time those notes had been developed, the ideas, images, thoughts and experiences have become poetry. (It has to be pointed out, though, that not every single one of Redgrove's poems escaped being derived in part from prose, and sometimes they could come across as prose broken up into verses. This was particularly noticeable in the pieces which derived from the same source in the journals).

Along with rhythm, Peter Redgrove employed many of the traditional techniques of poetry, such as alliteration, repetition, varying the length of lines, and so on. He does not use rhymes at the end of lines so much (more in the early poetry), but does employ internal rhymes and hints at rhyming within or across lines. Many of Redgrove's poems contain lines of twelve or more syllables, while just as many comprise half-lines of two or three feet. Formally, Redgrove favoured two and three line stanzas often, but also large groups of formal lines in stanzas of irregular length. Sometimes he mixed formal poetry with prose poetry (as in 'The Yoniversity At Rock', which has 3 stanzas of three lines in the first part, six stanzas of three lines in the second part, but a prose poem of 29 lines in the third part).

The 'sealed writing' was an aid to creative work which Redgrove taught his art students at Falmouth College of Art. A description of it appeared in *Alchemy For Women* and *The Black Goddess and the Sixth Sense*: it involved writing whatever came into one's head for twenty minutes at a relaxed time (before bed, say), regularly, over a period of, say, three months. But the writing wasn't looked at until much later (preferrably with a friend reading it out aloud). Then, amazing images and synæsthetic experiences could occur.

> Language, which can handle all the senses, thought and feeling too, clears like a magic mirror to the supersensible, which includes one's inner senses and further personality. (BG, 175)

The sealed writing was 'a form of controlled waking dreaming' (AFW, 43), a means of tapping into the unconscious. The sealed writing method never failed, Redgrove maintained, if followed properly, and could feed into all of one's creative work. Developed over time, one could also petition the unconscious, ask it questions: Redgrove suggested doing the same thing in dream or trance states (before going to sleep, say), and also in the post-orgasmic afterglow. One couldn't *demand* results from such trances, dreams or experiences, but one could politely ask.

Alongside the sealed writing and the artist's and writer's journal or notebook (which's still the centrepiece of art school education in Britain), Mr Redgrove suggested keeping a diary of one's dreams. These methods were part of Redgrove's notions of using the unconscious or dark senses or trances in creative work, and developing 'feedback' systems. One of the points Redgrove makes repeatedly is that the poet already has plenty of material s/he can use in her/ his work, without having to look too far.

3

Adventures in the Mother-World: Extra-Sensuous Perception

We are surrounded by invisibles, yet we ignore what is invisible, real, potent, natural.

Peter Redgrove, *The Black Goddess and the Sixth Sense* (xvii)

...this mother-world
Opened around me...

Peter Redgrove, 'The Case'[1]

3.1   The Sixth Sense

Peter Redgrove created a science of the strange, a mythology of natural mysteries, a poetry of synæsthetic experiences. Robert Graves produced his *The White Goddess* (1946), his own 'historical grammar of poetic myth'; Redgrove answered Graves's book with *The Black Goddess and the Sixth Sense* (1987). Graves began to write of the Black Goddess, the counter-part of his famous notion of the White Goddess, the Muse of poets, in the 1960s. In that decade, Graves wrote more poems than ever before. The new poems are marked by a belief in an ecstatic, timeless experience of love, a transcendent love, a love that is magical and joins lovers præternaturally over distances.[1] There isn't space here to get into Graves's fascinating biography, and the new women in Graves's life (not all of them lovers) who inspired Graves to eulogize the Black Goddess.

Robert Graves's new, miraculous form of loving is developed by Peter Redgrove in his *The Black Goddess and the Sixth Sense* to form a new way of experiencing life – through all the senses, and especially through the 'dark' or 'animal' senses (a.k.a. the 'sixth' sense), that of the Black Goddess, the unknown/ unconscious/ invisible. It is this dark realm of synæsthesia that Redgrove explored in his poetry.

Max Beckman, the greatest of German Expressionist painters, spoke of wanting to make the invisible visible, his aim being 'always to get hold of the magic of reality'.[2] This is Redgrove's aim also.

The breakthrough for Peter Redgrove came with the poetry of *In the Country of the Skin,* later worked into a novel and radio play. Redgrove is a poet first and foremost – the other things – essays, novels, plays – are 'cooler', being further away from the 'hot' centre, which is the poems. 'The bright water unites our skins', Redgrove wrote in *In the Country of the Skin* (36).

What happens is that Redgrove experienced and perceived in a heightened way, the way normally suppressed by contemporary culture, the states of perception called 'altered states of consciousness' in the 1960s. These states or experiences include dreams, yogic bliss, meditation, relaxation, hypnosis, the afterglow of orgasm, etc. As he said: '[a]ll of my poetry is really about waking up after sex.'[3] It's about exploring 'that state of hypnotic openness of floating in and out of sleep', with each partner telling the other about their dreams, creating 'a kind of mutual feed-back hypnosis' with images altering, blending, interacting (AFW, 121). This kind of 'sex magic' is 'often no other than introducing images into such a reverie' (WW, 162). Dubbed the 'cosmic orgasm' by women's magazines such as *Cosmopolitan*, Redgrove described the feeling as a kind of Zen enlightenment, a lightening of the body akin to religious conversion:

> a wonderful feeling of well-being, combined with sharpness of perception and deepness of thought-feeling. The orgasm eroticizes the world for both partners. It is timeless, egoless, and in continuum with nature. (AFW, 137-8)

In 'With This Wolf I Thee Wed' (great title), Redgrove called it the 'gulf orgasm', an orgasm which altered 'the balance of senses', and 'opened gulfs', a move into limitlessness and heightened perception (CM, 14). As US writer Marco Vassi put it in *The Erotic Comedies* (another writer who celebrates eroticism to the max): 'orgasm is *the* life-enchancing process'. For Vassi,

> To fuck with someone one is romantically in love with is undoubtedly the most exhilarating form of metasex. There is a totality, a joy, an overall sensation of rapture unparalleled in the other modes. (134, 197)

The aim is to cultivate a state of acute awareness, of right attention to the world, as Oriental mystics put it. Openness, not closure. Awareness, not dullness. Inner and outer coalesce (it's not just enhanced subjectivity and interiority, not just a sinking down into oneself, culminating in an autistic self-absorption, a flight from reality: it is ultimately aimed at experiencing the outside world – and other people – deeper).

Here's an example of what Redgrove is after, from *In the Esplumeor: An Alchemical Journal* (no. 7):

> ...after that to stroke her skin like a cat's so it emits her perfume which combines with mine and fills the whole house with its radiance; and compounds with the radiance and perfume of the flowers, *lumen de lumine*, an electrochemical field, respirable gold, the fruits of the swift tree of life of the lightning, rooted in the sky,

blossoming on earth.

Each Redgrovean subject (bees, clouds, honey, stars, seas, storms) is treated in this heightened, multi-sensory fashion. But what marks Redgrove's poetry from other poetry is not so much his subjects – after all, other poets write about skies and storms, for example – but the golden alchemical light he throws around everything, so that things 'shine' with this accentuated awareness and mythopœic openness. Take 'The Brilliance', or 'Visibility Nil', or 'The Alchemical Honeymoon' (all printed here). Each of those poems is alive with a multi-sensory awareness, so that a fly crawling over a page can be a fascinating starting-point for a poem, or a drenched white shirt. Like all poets, Redgrove constantly makes intuitive connections between things. Between the perfume of a woman after sex radiating in a room and the smell of a lawn before rain.

In *The Alchemical Journal* (published as *In the Esplumeor: An Alchemical Journal* in *The Cyclopean Mistress*), a myriad of perceptions are unified by the poet's alchemical pellucidity. Each prose-poem chains together sensations and visions in a single paragraph: see no. 33, which links together mines, the moon, light, stone, and mothers and daughters:

> Under the black light, mother and daughter, in Poldark Mine, near Helston, the room lined with shelves full of the crystalline minerals bathed in ultra-violet, shining their unnamed colours, like solid fireworks slowly exploding, the mother and daughter, the faces black but the radiant white calcite of the teeth luminous as the million year lump of calcite aglow beside them, the light's tunes played on the rocks, the nails bright in the black hands like night reaching out of the bluely-luminous ocean-foaming sleeves.

'Like' is a word and idea Peter Redgrove employed continuously: poetry as eternal metaphor. So black hands are 'like night', colours are 'like feelings', a chapel organ vibrates 'like a river', waves are 'like great invisible personages', gloves are 'like hypnotised doves', speech is 'like the weather', and so on (all of these examples are from the sections

SEX–MAGIC–POETRY–CORNWALL

in *In the Esplumeor* immediately following No. 33).

The Black Goddess and the Sixth Sense is a poet's handbook, exactly like Robert Graves's *The White Goddess* (pagans, musicians, filmmakers and artists have cited *The White Goddess* as an useful sourcebook, as well as poets). Both books set out in a highly concentrated form – like the juice pressed from ripe fruit. Graves and Redgrove collected together all those poetic problems, sensations, ideas, observations and obsessions that have fascinated them for so long. Both books are quirky and highly individual: Redgrove's *Black Goddess* contains far more science and rational thinking than Graves's *White Goddess* (Graves was suspicious of such non-poetic thought), but it is as idiosyncratic as Graves's tome (however, Graves loved to show off his obscure research, and his etymological flourishes). These are the works of poets who've delved long and deep into the backgrounds behind and underneath poetry and the poetic life. And both *The White Goddess* and *The Black Goddess and the Sixth Sense* have the format and flavour of personal treatises. They're about the pleasures and costs of being a poet, of following the poetic vocation (which both Graves and Redgrove, like Francesco Petrarch and William Shakespeare, say, took seriously). The sense of committment to the poetic life comes across very strongly in both books (Graves was probably more monk-like and Puritanical in his devotion to the poetic life than Redgrove; he does harp on it like a preacher at times. And Graves certainly didn't go for the same explicit eroticism. There are no references to clitorises or 'cunt dew' in Graves's poetry).

One can dip into *The White Goddess* anywhere, and discover something useful or unusual. Similarly with *The Black Goddess*, which is intended as a second book in a trilogy about poetry, feminine mysteries, mythology and multi-sensory experiences. The first book was *The Wise Wound*. Redgrove told me in the early Nineties that the third book was having problems getting published – due, he said, to its subject matter of women and menstruation. He thought that the establishment didn't know quite what to make of his poetic and psychological explorations of menstruation and women's mysteries. He showed me the manuscript of *The Menstrual Mandala* or *Creative Menstruation* (as it was then titled). When it appeared in 1995 as *Alchemy For Women*, it was a somewhat different book (the word 'menstruation', which publishers were wary of, didn't appear on the cover or title page for instance. Instead, the subtitle was: *Personal Transformation Through Dreams and the Female Cycle*). Since then, more books have been published which considered the same territory.

Appearing in the mid-1990s, *Alchemy For Women* became part of the self-help, Mind/ Body/ Spirit genre (Redgrove and Shuttle had been linked to that movement since the 1970s). *Alchemy For Women* contained all of the usual Redgrovean preoccupations: with menstruation and dream psychology, creative work, and sexual practices. Redgrove and Shuttle explored the links between the menstrual cycle and popular culture, with horror films being a favourite topic; one of the best and most entertaining chapters of *The Wise Wound*, "The Mirror of Dracula", is the discussion of classic horror movies in terms of menstruation and blood mysteries, You won't look at Christopher Lee and Peter Cushing in the Hammer horrors, or *The Exorcist*, or *Rosemary's Baby*, the same way again. It's an excellent deconstruction of monsters, vampires, demons and ghosts.

There are also plenty of explorations in *Alchemy For Women* of practices and belief systems such as yoga, hypnosis, mesmerism, alchemy, split brain psychology, Bach flower remedies, homeopathy, aromatherapy, acupuncture, reflexology, relaxation, massage, sealed writing, T'ai Chi, Tantric sex magic, Taoism, fetishism, witchcraft, Christianity, and so on. And everyday activities, such as cooking, gardening, walking, diet, and the weather. (Many of these preoccupations had been explored in *The Wise Wound* and *The Black Goddess and the Sixth Sense*, and some of *Alchemy For Women* reprinted whole sections of *The Black Goddess*).

As well as the familiar pursuits of 'New Age' or self-help or alternative therapy culture like massage or T'ai Chi, Redgrove and Shuttle also recommended simple things like dehumidifiers and negative ion generators to liven up the home environment, or taking aspirin and having a rest.

One of the primary goals of *Alchemy For Women* was helping people (men, women and children) to live with the menstrual cycle. So it wasn't only women who were the intended audience of the book, but also men living with women (but women were the primary audience). For Redgrove and Shuttle, it was vital that men learn how to live with their partner's menstrual cycle: 'men must work in all respects with their *Soror Alchymica*, 'Alchemical Sister'', they wrote (61).

Dreams were the key to unlocking the energies and anxieties of the cycle for Shuttle and Redgrove: the way in was getting in tune with one's dreams, and plotting them on a 'menstrual mandala', a chart of each month, as the cycle moved from ovulation to menstruation and back to ovulation. Men have biological and dream cycles, too, and if they fall into the same shape as the woman's, it can reduce her menstrual distress, according to Shuttle and Redgrove (68).

The mandalas themselves divided the 28 days of the menstrual cycle into four quarters of seven days: from the period at day 4 through pre-ovulation (follicle ripens; ovum descends), to ovulation at day 18, through post-ovulation (corpus luteum peaks), to pre-menstruation. It was a cycle of continuous birth and regeneration, moving through conflicts and thresholds, a pattern of ripening and receding (AFW, 32). Dreams, relaxation exercises, sealed writing, massage and other techniques were a way of moving through the menstrual cycle positively, learning how to recognize and use the painful or problematic experiences.

Alchemy For Women wasn't an illustrated self-help book, the kind which have been popular for many years (some menstrual mandalas were included), but it did contain all sorts of useful information about relaxation exercises, yoga, homeopathy, (self-)hypnosis, meditation, left and right brain psychology, massage, acupuncture, Tantrism, physical exercises (but not competitive exercise), breathing exercises (such as alternate nostril breathing), gardening, and so on. Most of these Redgrove and Shuttle called different types of yogas.

And the highest, most potent form of yoga was lovemaking. So a chapter of *Alchemy For Women* was devoted to exploring sex yoga, using lovemaking for relaxation, for creative work, to help with dreams, or anxieties, and so on. Familiar Redgrovean concerns – such as developing women's multi-orgasmic potential and 'the 'ladder' or 'staircase' of orgasms' – were explored. So, in its idiosyncratic fashion, *Alchemy For Women* was an addition to a genre which featured *The Joy of Sex* (Redgrove was of the same generation and mind-set as Alex Comfort), books on yoga or meditation, video and DVD guides to better lovemaking, books on Tantric or Oriental sex, Deepak Chopra videos, and even the wave of witchcraft publishing aimed at young women (and TV shows like *Charmed*, *Buffy* and *Hex*, and movies such as *Practical Magic*, *Bewitched*, *The Witches of Eastwick* and *The Craft*).

Peter Redgrove in *The Black Goddess* spoke of all-over perception, feeling with the whole skin (a total skin feeling was a recurring Redgrovean motif). He discussed skin at length – of potentials, currents, electricity, etc (96f). Redgrove is the poet who told readers what they already secretly knew: that rain is an orgasm:

> The outdoors working in the rain
> In the thundershower leads to
> What we shall call a skin orgasm,
> the whole world turned to glass.
> (from 'Glassworking' [Tar, 9])

The idea of rain being erotic is nothing new: the ancient agriculturalists of the Near East certainly knew – and exalted – the sacred links between sexuality, fertility, growth, the seasons and the earth – and women.[4] So rain could be seen by poets as the orgasm of the Goddess, a nourishing flood of juice from the womb of the world.

When the Redgrove-poet is writing about 'juice' or 'elixir' or 'dew' he means the womb's wetness or 'cunt dew' (and recommends that both partners mix and kiss the woman's elixir, as a way of aiding menstrual distress). There are two kinds of love juice in Redgrove's mythopœia: the red love juice of menstruation and the white liquid of ovulation, the childless and the child-giving (WW, 21). In the poem 'Alchemy At the Couturier's', for instance, Redgrove writes:

> After this drink
> Of dragon-womb elixir
> Of Grandee woman
> I step forward like a new-clothed man. (OE, 47)

3.2 Clouds

Let's start with clouds. Hardly any poet has written so evocatively (or so often) of clouds. Yet how crucial clouds are! Without clouds, how flat and uneventful the sky – and part of life – would be. Clouds bring weather, and rain, and without rain there would be no humans. That's how vital rain is.

Rain's far more important than God.

Clouds are at once everyday and wonderful phenomena. So it is great to find a poet like Peter Redgrove writing passionately about clouds. And not just about the sight of them, but of their physical properties, their ionization, their electrostatic qualities, etc. Of clouds at Land's-End, Redgrove wrote in *The Black Goddess and the Sixth Sense*:

> There are shadows and tones in my thought which alter as the clouds alter, but which seem to be sustained also by the drum-beat under my feet. I look at my companion, and she alters too in this glamour, as I realise too that I see more and feel it as a direct consequence of her being present. She glows a little. At least I think

she does, but it is difficult to separate this perception (even if I wanted to) from the knowledge that we have a short time ago been making love. I know that this has sensitised us, and we have been re-tuned by orgasm to all that we see and feel now; our skins have an altered pattern of heat and electricity and are differently reacting to one another's reactions, like the amplifications inside that resonant laser-chamber of the cloud, not just on the verbal level or by caress. (BG, 112-3).

In Redgrove's multiverse, clouds are 'ice cathedrals' which resonate over people, and people give back feelings to them. So as the clouds float by, humans interact with them – physiologically as well as emotionally. There are many, many poems to clouds, rain, storms, thunder, lightning and weather working in the Redgroverse: 'Rain on Vaux Hill', 'Round Pylons', 'Glassmaking', 'Odour of Magnetism', 'A Maze Like Us', 'Air', 'Superstition', 'Weather', 'The Pale Brows of Lightning', 'Whitsunwind', 'Transactions' and 'Cloud-Rustling', to name but a few of the best poems.

This cloud-sensibility is nothing new in Redgrove's poesie – one of his earliest collections, *The Nature of Cold Weather*, contains poems about ghostly, nighttime mists, for example ('Mists'). The electricity and energy of storms informs so much of Redgrove's poetic outlook. The storm is the energy of life itself, whether one calls it 'the Moon', or 'the Goddess', or 'God', or 'Tao', or 'spirit', or whatever. Look at the wonderful 'A Maze Like Us', which speaks of 'serpent-lightning streaks, the fire-snake':

> The lightning zig-zags through its maze.
> The thunderbird takes feathers of blue flame,
> Flaps immense shadows in his mountain aviary
> Of clouds, immense lightnings
> Among the heaped water, the heavenly
> Cisterns with their gunpowder disposition
> That are in this moment sapphire,
>
> This moment, ebony scented with electricity.
> There is a darkness that reveals other lights

SEX–MAGIC–POETRY–CORNWALL

Present in this thunderstorm, present in the mother
Of clouds. (IHS, 31)

Storms of course are fantastic sensual experiences, veritable orgasmic 'skin orgasms'. Redgrove devotes many pages of his book *The Black Goddess and the Sixth Sense* to storms, maintaining that storms can be very creative (BG, 78f). Air pressure, temperature, wind direction and speed, rainfall, and so on affects people whether they realize it or not. Redgrove is fascinated not only by the effect of changes in climate on people, but how they affect creativity. In the poem 'A Dewy Garment' Redgrove speaks of 'the film a black-and-white thunderstorm | Flashing eighteen times a second' (IHS, 27).

One imagines that Redgrove would enjoy the American land artist Walter de Maria's *Lightning Field* (1977), which is a grid of steel poles, each two inches in diameter, 18 feet high, 30 feet apart from each other, set in five rows of seven in the Arizonan desert. De Maria's piece of land art attracts lightning during the storm season, and is a very impressive installation during lightning strikes.

Storms can be highly erotic (when they're not creating floods and destroying towns), and when Peter Redgrove is writing about a storm in a poem he is also writing of the feminine mysteries, of the Goddess. For him, the 'whole-body' sensation of the weather is linked to the orgasmic state. So one often finds women in his storms in his poems, or wet garments, which also point towards a charged eroticism. There's an eroticism of nature in most nature mysticism and poetry – in Friedrich Hölderlin, Samuel Taylor Coleridge, Heinrich Heine, William Shakespeare. For Redgrove, the body is a weather system in itself, as is a house: '[f]amilies create living vessels of alchemy in their homes, distilling human weather from room to room' he writes (BG, 68). And many people are acutely weather-sensitive, causing depressions, tensions, electrical charges. and other physiological effects, as people react to high and low pressure systems.

Peter Redgrove's point is that there is a scientific, physiological basis for such commonplace notions such as the 'atmosphere' of a room, or the way the weather affects humans. Cornwall features prominently in Redgrove's mythology of weather and the 'skin orgasm', because the weather is so changeable in Falmouth (BG, xi), and the nearby Lizard peninsula creates weather, he says in the poem 'Weather Begins Here (Cornwall)': '[m]uch of the weather of England is born on Goonhilly Downs' (AB, 12). And Cornwall is linked to China and Chinese art: so that Cornish poets don't write *about* thunder, rain, clouds and cats as *by means* of them (FVC, 76).

Redgrove saw himself as living in a series of interconnecting alchemical vessels. First there is the alchemical womb of his lover; then the vessel of her body, in which every tumultuous – or delicate – change in the weather of the cosmos occurs; then there is the alchemical vessel of the house, which is a laboratory with many interconnected rooms; then there is Falmouth; then Cornwall; then the sea; then the whole universe. Lastly, and importantly, there is the chemical/ alchymical vessel of his poetry, in which every other alchemical vessel is joined together by magical correspondences and dream visions.

This is from 'Alchemy At the Couturier's', published in 1997:

> Laboratory fits into laboratory.
> The inmost vessel is the woman's vessel
> Who directs her laborators
> From the desires of that vessel
> Like a canopied temple of veils
> Parted by the woman emerging
> Into her domain
> Of magnified cunt
> Which is silks of all kinds
> Seen swathed in mirrors
> Like fields of magnetism
> Of lamés slashed with gold,
> The flaying of dragons,
> The new suit of dragon-pelt;
> Assistants pat and tack. (OE, 46)

SEX–MAGIC–POETRY–CORNWALL

Peter Redgrove is always talking about magical spaces, the laboratory, *temenos*, womb, moon-place, Merlin's 'esplumeor' (a term that fascinated John Cowper Powys's John Geard in *A Glastonbury Romance*). Merlin has fascinated British poets for centuries. Redgrove's exploration of the cage or or room or 'esplumeor' in the Merlin legend is part of a long tradition of ruminations in poetry and fiction of the Arthurian wizard. John Cowper Powys, Robert Nye, Nikolai Tolstoy, Mary Stewart, John Matthews and many others have focussed on the figure of Merlin the magician. and Merlin is a big influence on *The Lord of the Rings* and *Harry Potter*.

Robert Graves spoke of the poem as creating a 'magic ring' around the reader.[1] Each poem is a magic circle or a womb-place where transformations can occur. For Redgrove, a poem must create experiences as well as 'record' or 'describe' them. This notion of feedback works on a physiological as well as psychic level (these ideas are discussed in *The Wise Wound*). In a piece on his 1981 poetry book *The Apple-Broadcast*, Redgrove explains this notion of the poem giving back something:

> It is currently held that a poem must arise out of experience. True enough, but only half the story. A poem must also *give* you an experience… The poem is a tuning or feedback device which alters or adjusts our capacity to respond to the world.[2]

Readers do more than intellectually digest a poem when they 'read' it (feedback is one of Redgrove's recurring concerns). Cultural/ postmodernist theory has demonstrated how crucial 'reading' is. Reading becomes writing: one 'writes' (creates) one's own texts as one interacts with texts (what Roland Barthes called the 'pleasure of the text'). One 're-writes' 'Shakespeare' as one 'reads' the Bard's plays or poems. Redgrove is arguing for a *physiological* foundation for this feedback, as well as a cultural, psychological or emotional one, terming it biofeedback.

Painters know about these things, of course, when they chose particular colours. It is well-known, for example, that the colour orange increases the heartbeat and raises blood pressure.[3] And linguists know that the mouth and vocal cords move when people 'speak' aloud in their minds – their bodies react to words, physically.[4] And the different levels of speaking are well-known: silently, in the head, or aloud, in the head, or with the voice. And when you add the spoken voice to poetry, it becomes really extraordinary (Redgrove has a poem about this: 'The Girl Reading My Poetry' [IHS, 29]).

Redgrove argues for all the neglected senses (which he calls the 'dark', 'non-visual' or 'invisible' senses). He writes: 'our eyes see the rain, but our whole bodies feel it is raining – it touches us, its music sounds on roads and buildings' (BG, 92). Blind people have described rainfall as a wonderful way in which a landscape is made graspable – how the *sound* of rain falling enriches the apprehension of an environment. Cultivating the non-visual senses means

> becoming curious about magic or about everything feminine and individual, watching for one's intuitions and dreams, becoming interested in the lore of the night and the moon, becoming interested in 'primary process' – everything primitive, archaic, vivid, immediate, child-like, sensuous... (AFW, 102)

What happens in Redgrove's poesie stems largely from the post-orgasmic state: he and his lover go out walking after lovemaking, and the world is perceived in a fresh way, as if after a storm, the air lucid, the perfumes of the world newly intoxicating. Redgrove says:

> We find that if we go to bed at night, make love, dream, and sit down for breakfast the next morning, there erupts an amazing firework of pleasure in life: the senses have been cleaned, the world transformed' (Met)

The juices and essences of orgasm, exchanged by the lovers and studied by Taoist 'Love Masters', become the rain-filled streets and the clouds above. The weather of the bodies conjoined in orgasm becomes the weather of the whole house and, by extension – because poetic magic is all-inclusive – the whole world. See the essences being exchanged in

SEX–MAGIC–POETRY–CORNWALL

'Cornwall Honeymoon', a poem which as much about the Cornish landscape as it is about love and eroticism. Indeed, these things are the same: the landscape, the lovescape, the sexscape. One can speak of the 'landscapes of love' in Peter Redgrove's poetry, for his landscapes are filled with erotic feeling, as 'Cornwall Honeymoon' shows powerfully:

> After the bath
> She blazed with beauty. The crane of the docks
> Like a fire-escape to heaven, a staircase
> Of steel into the sky, I will see it
>
> Magnificently wreathed in ivy. The eyes
> Meeting in orgasm, the salty breath exchanged,
> The kaolin waters of the man and woman mingling... (Man, 17)

The imagery of Redgrove's poetry fuses: light, storms, stars, oceans, black/ white, water, glass, clothes, etc. Thomas Hardy would say that he walked to his beloved to see her, but Redgrove changes this: 'I *rainwalked* to Annalee in Lower Lodestone'.[5] The term 'rainwalked' changes the sense of walking entirely. It becomes a Powysian walk, where walking is a series of ecstasies. (There is a clue, too, in that place, 'Lower Lodestone' – the word 'lower' refers, as in 'nether' of 'Nether Powers', to the erotic, dark underlife of things). (In *Alchemy For Women*, Redgrove calls walking a useful form of yoga [139]).

In Thomas Hardy's world, nature mysticism is of the traditional kind: Gabriel Oak under the wheeling stars in *Far From the Madding Crowd*; Tess Durbeyfield in the ethereal dawns of Talbothays; in *The Woodlanders,* Giles Winterbourne has a sacred relation with the trees; and in so many poems the Hardyan suitor wanders over the Dorsetshire hills to see his betrothed so many times, pausing at every graveyard along the way to scrutinize the tombstones.

All this nature poetry is familiar. It is the standard English poetic response to nature, found in the writings of William Wordsworth, Percy Shelley, Edmund Spenser, John Donne, etc. But in the work of Redgrove – and in the art of Powys, Rainer Maria Rilke, St-John Perse, Arthur

SEX–MAGIC–POETRY–CORNWALL

Rimbaud and others – sensuality is of a different order. In Redgrove's *œuvre*, God is not found in the workings of the universe – there is no Prime Mover, no Creator, or whatever, as in the world of William Wordsworth or Jacob Boehme. There is, simply, the incredible, intoxicating reality of the thing-in-itself (something Rilke and the Existential philosophers such as Martin Heidegger and Jean-Paul Sartre tried to get at when they spoke of *innigkeit,* or *dasein,* or 'isness', or 'thereness', as Zen Buddhists might say).

For poets, the thing-in-itself, the thereness of the world, must be primary. So there is the cloud. The tree. The apple. The ocean. So a rain shower can be a 'skin orgasm' or, in the poem 'Living in Falmouth', a fall of dreams:

> Clouds-dreams let loose a moment of shower,
> Dream-tides knock the fencing dream-boats
> And two-legged dreams make one flesh. (SP, 127)

3.3 Sex/ Weather/ Clothes/ Body

It's clear by now that Peter Redgrove's poetic relation with the world is erotic (if not always erotic, then sensual in large part). For him, weather is erotic; nature is erotic; the landscape is erotic; and poetry streams from the orgasmic state. So Redgrove will speak of the sexuality of the weather, and the meteorological quality of sex (while feminists and cultural theorists speak of 'the sexuality of texts' and 'the textuality of sex').[1] In the poem 'Field Theory', Redgrove wrote:

> The vast slow weather-whirlpool turns
> And rustles like a young woman's rainy clothes.
>
> There is a great white ear floating high up there,

SEX–MAGIC–POETRY–CORNWALL

Listening; then the white hunter comes
Sliding with his buckler through the night:

Orion. Morning: the daisy-lawn
Photographs the sun in holograms
With its yellow core and white influence

Stretching over the sky, and the green stem
Swivelling. (AB, 32)

If Peter Redgrove has a fetishized object, it is surely a 'young woman's rainy clothes'. Nothing turns him on more than a drenched white blouse. With Thomas Hardy, it was the rustle of a woman's dress on a heath; for John Cowper Powys, it was a young sylph's slender limbs (particularly the ankles); for André Gide it was a young Arab boy; for Francesco Petrarch it was Laura's eyes that drove him mad.

Apart from the womb of a woman, Redgrove eroticizes her clothes more than anything else. So many poems are devoted to wet clothes, to the 'shining nakedness' underneath 'stained garments' (CM, 44), to those 'wonder-awakening dresses' as he calls them in 'Wardrobe Lady':

She wears the long series of wonder-awakening dresses,
She wears the fishskin cloak,
She wears the gown with the constellations slashed into its dark
    lining,
She undresses out of the night sky, each night of the year a
    different sky,
She wears altitude dresses and vertigo dresses,
She plucks open the long staircase at the neck with the big
    buttons of bird-skulls in the white dress of sow-thistle.
She has leather britches known to be chimp-skin,
She has combed star-rays into a shaggy night-dress,
She has a bodice of bone-flounces, a turbinal blouse through
    which the air pours. (SP, 83)

The origin of the 'wonder-awakening' quality of the dresses is Penelope Shuttle, Redgrove's Muse. She wore these dresses when Redgrove met her back in the early 1970s. There are many poems to

Shuttle's clothes in the Redgroverse. In "Philosopher and Skin", one of *Eight Alcameos*, he wrote of '[p]lenty of wet girls in the mountains, clothed in goddess-skin of mist and waterfall' (EA, 139).

For Redgrove, wet women's clothes signify the height of synæsthetic experience. They seem to be related to the veils and membranes that swaddled the baby in the womb, and to the sensual powers of the skin (like being naked in the rain). Clothes-poems of Redgrove's include 'A Dewy Garment', 'Her Shirt Open', 'Mad Speech Concerning Dress', 'Pneumonia Blouses', 'Dress' and 'Night Light').

In many of Redgrove's poems of clothes, the dresses and blouses are the lining of the womb, the woman's sexuality worn over her skin, as if she had been opened inside out, but softly, full of liquid. Redgrove calls this 'exterior cunt', relating it to Luce Irigaray's notion of women's eroticism being 'all over' the body, a 'hysterization' of the skin. Wet, Redgrove's clothes are acutely touch-sensitive. So in the poem 'Dress', Redgrove wrote:

> ...let this dress register your sweat,
> Your cunt-musk and over its bodice your tears... (Tar, 24)

Clothes are crucial in Peter Redgrove's sensualism, because they cover the skin, which is, as he reminds readers, the largest organ of the body. If Redgrove had his way, everyone'd all go 'skyclad', as witches do at their festivals. Then, naked, folk would feel the air, the wind, the rain, every change in temperature, and the electrostasis and ionization of the clouds. As he says in the poem 'Childstone': 'I can hear better when I am naked' (Tar, 51). You know what he means.

So nude moments, such as having a bath, or swimming (as well as making the beast with two backs), are important. Skin-on-skin is a deep desire of Redgrove's: he writes in the poem 'Mad Speech Concerning Dress':

>   My skin
> Needs all skin, his and hers,

SEX–MAGIC–POETRY–CORNWALL

All at once, woven in one stuff, the many faces
Folding into one Countenance. (AB, 123)

Again and again in Peter Redgrove's multiverse, one sees the desire for unity, for wholeness. He is always talking of the *whole* house, the *whole* body, the *whole* world. This desire stems from a belief in the unity of things, which is perhaps the primary idea of magic. And it's the *whole* skin, the *totality* of skin, skin as the body's all-over organ. In the poem 'Mortier Water-Organ Called Oscar' (one of Redgrove's poems about unusual machines or structures), the Redgrove-poet speaks of:

Two skins in bed
Watching each other
Through the one skin
They have made... (OE, 50)

In *The Black Goddess and the Sixth Sense*, Redgrove created a poetry of clothes. He spoke of clothes as able to control the weather systems of the body – the blouse opening at the neck controls the air and scent and so on flowing around the body (BG, 66f). By opening her shirt, a woman can make the world magical. This is the latent meaning of the poem 'Her Shirt Open', where even a 'slate-lined alley' becomes '[e]rotic and holy':

She opens her shirt, which is wet
And heavy with its drink like a superb silk,
And an eerie feeling superimposes
From the stone electricity and that vertical smile,
Like another music, or echoes
Exploring buildings not yet visible,
The metallic echoes of the slate-lined alley
Erotic and holy, as when we watched
The slow-growing sea-drowned grass
And she turned to me again, her shirt open,
And the current changed around us, and in the canal
The underwater forests switched direction
Showing that sluices far away had opened up
New reaches of the waterway, with varying tides. (IHS, 10)

SEX–MAGIC–POETRY–CORNWALL

Redgrove's poetry of clothes makes garments extraordinary – but not in the flashy, materialistic, superficial way of the fashion industry and multi-national corporations (the commodified, postmodern, digital body of late consumer capitalism).

3.4 Magic

There is something huge, vast and infinite in Peter Redgrove's poetic cosmos, usually symbolized by the stars, sea and clouds. Redgrove uses the basic tenet of magic – *as above, so below* – which comes from the Emerald Table of Hermes Trismegistus.[1] Basically, the hermetic mantra says that everything on Earth reflects everything in Heaven. Or, more accurately and psychologically, inner and outer are connected, even identical. In second wave feminism (which's Redgrove's form of feminism), the personal was political. So the intimate, private orgasmic union of two lovers in the Redgroverse is seen as identical with public, worldly energies like weather, communities, societies and nature. This is fundamental to Western magic, this sense of unity in all things, so the stars can influence human lives (in astrology), or certain colours can influence certain acts, or certain herbs can help certain emotions to be produced, etc. The basic theory of magical correspondences, famously and elegantly expressed by Charles Baudelaire in his poem 'Correspondances', occurs throughout Western art – in William Shakespeare's plays, in mediæval alchemy, in Neoplatonism, and in Oriental mysticisms such as Taoism, where the Tao is the Way and the One, something akin to 'the One' of Neoplatonism.

> La Nature est un temple où de vivants piliers
> Laissent parfois sortir de confuses paroles;
> L'homme y passe à travers des forêts de symboles

SEX–MAGIC–POETRY–CORNWALL

Qui l'observent avec des regards familiers.
Comme de longs échos qui de loin se confondent
Dans une ténébreuse et profonde unité,
Vaste comme la nuit et comme la clarté,
Les parfums, les couleurs et les sons se répondent.

Il est des parfums frais comme des chairs d'enfants,
Doux comme les hautbois, verts comme les prairies,
— Et d'autres, corrompus, riches et triomphants,

Ayant l'expansion des choses infinies,
Comme l'ambre, le musc, le benjoin et l'encens,
Qui chantent les transports de l'esprit et des sens.[2]

Peter Redgrove's is a poetry of correspondences in the manner of Baudelaire and Rimbaud, as is all poetry. So a woman's body can be her house (in *In the Esplumeor: An Alchemical Journal*), or the touch of a lover can be like the caress of the stars. Inner and outer commingle. Redgrove's system of poetic correspondences is part of the alternative beliefs to traditional Western religion: alchemy, astrology, cheiromancy, geomancy, Gnosticism, witchcraft, angelism, Rosicrucianism, Neoplatonism – all those cults, movements and beliefs which form the 'underbelly' of Western religion, which seem to be in opposition to Judaism, Islam and Christianity, but which in fact fuse with Islamic-Judæo-Christianity at many points. These beliefs are 'occult' but normal – that is, they occur everywhere but are suppressed or hidden away.

Starting with weather – an agreeably neutral topic (though not really neutral at all) – Peter Redgrove showed in his study *The Black Goddess and the Sixth Sense* that so many 'occult' or 'supernatural' experiences are in fact normal. Redgrove took the magic founded by Dionysius the Areopagite, Dante Alighieri, Cornelius Agrippa, Paracelsus, John Dee, the *Qabbalah*, Sufic mysticism, Gnosticism, Plato, Aristotle, Pythagoras, Hermes Trismegistus, etc, and made it homely. That is, he brought it into the home, instead of leaving it in the secret laboratory, or on the windswept hilltop, or the Freemasons Lodge, or the coven in the glade of some far-distant forest.

SEX–MAGIC–POETRY–CORNWALL

In poetry's 'theory of correspondences' (what Charles Baudelaire called the 'forest of symbols'), everything connects together. So initiates can move, intuitively (poetically) from angels to planets to plants to numbers to jewels to minerals to humours to days to colours to elements to planets and round and round again. Sections of Redgrove's *Alchemical Journal* (*In the Esplumeor*) are pure magic – see no. 15, for example:

> Bricks in Staines, the small Roman bricks, numerous as the leaves on the trees, a world of smells and angels, angels behind their wings of smell, the smell of an angel wafted to me by the soft movement of its wings, says the Book of Lambsprink, and, my hammers are the seven planets with which I forge beautiful things. The fire of our stars lies hidden in our substances.

There is more alchemy, magic, hermeticism and conscious symbol-making in Peter Redgrove's poetry than in most modern poets. One thinks of W.B. Yeats and Robert Graves, forerunners of Redgrove's generation, who both created magical poetic systems. Graves's work can happily be read without needing notes, but it helps enormously in the depth of understanding of his poems if readers can also dip into *The White Goddess* (which acts as a handbook to Graves's poetry). It's a question of levels, how deep one wishes to go. It's the same with Redgrove's art. Although he terms all his poetry as strange-but-ordinary, it does help if one knows something of magic, occultism and psychology.

In the 20th century, it was C.G. Jung who probably did more to bring together magic, mysticism, religion, psychology and science than any other individual (one thinks also of writers like J.G. Frazer, Jessie Weston, Mircea Eliade, Sigmund Freud, Erich Neumann and Gaston Bachelard). In Jung's marvellous *Collected Works*, readers can leap from subjects such as mediæval Gnosticism to Chinese alchemy, or from the psychology of *animus* possession to the *Book of Job*. Redgrove follows in this wide-ranging Jungian tradition. Redgrove's philosophy is firmly in the Jung-Eliade-Layard tradition.

There are three worlds or states of being in Peter Redgrove's

SEX–MAGIC–POETRY–CORNWALL

mythopœia:

World	Imagery
Upper, higher, transcendent realm	stars, clouds, ocean, wind
Middle, day-to-day realm	people, societies, events
Lower, underworld, 'underlife'	'dark senses', sex, orgasm, yoga

The poet is the shaman who unites these three realms of heaven, earth and underworld. The archaic shaman of prehistory climbed the World Tree, the Cosmic Tree or *axis mundi* which links the three ontological realms. The poet travels between the worlds. Look at Rainer Maria Rilke, Arthur Rimbaud, Homer or Dante Alighieri – you'll see them making these spiritual journeys all the time.[3] What Redgrove was trying to do was to join the three realms together, so that the higher, celestial or transcendent realm is not off-limits like the Judæo-Christian heaven, something to be experienced after death (if you're lucky), but to bring it into the everyday world, to pull heaven down from the clouds and stars and bring it into the home, into everyday life. Similarly, that dark, chthonic under-realm, presided over by the Black Goddess, the Muse or lover, is also brought into everyday spaces. Poetry, the creative act (and love) melts these realms together. So everything is pulled in, by the electromagnetism of poetry, into the womb-space, into the cauldron of the Goddess, into the alchemical vessel which is the womb (the world) of the beloved woman.

So poetry is essential in the manufacture of a life. It is essential to make art because art can join together all experiences, all zones, all ontologies. Or, if not art, then meditate, or make love, or do something creative (the creative act in its broadest sense is the key to Redgrove's life-philosophy). For the poet and writer, one must write – always – as the French feminist Hélène Cixous said in her essay "The Laugh of the Medusa", which was probably one of the most important feminist texts for Redgrove, and for many feminists, because it is so energizing and

SEX–MAGIC–POETRY–CORNWALL

inspiring. 'Why don't you write? Write! Writing is for you, you are for you... Write, let no one hold you back, let nothing stop you'.[4]

For Cixous (who is loved and loathed by feminists nearly as energetically as Andrea Dworkin or Germaine Greer or Princess Diana), writing is absolutely crucial, and central. Cixous asserted that

> writing, writing poetically, treating language as one of the most important things in the world, today sounds mad. Yet for human beings it is the first most important thing.[5]

Writing is oxygen to Cixous, she must write to live, as she says:

> Having never been without writing, having writing in my body, at my throat, on my lips... to me my texts are elements of a whole which interweaves my own story.[6]

Cixous writes of a writing which is desperate, which risks the really important things in life, which the writer needs to write in order to keep alive.[7] Cixous, in *Three Steps On the Ladder of Writing* (1993), wrote eloquently of the poetic act, and likens it to movement, in particular walking, and sex – the body in action:

> Walking, dancing, pleasure: these accompany the poetic act. I wonder what kind of poet doesn't wear out their shoes, writes with their head. The true poet is a reveller. Poetry is about travelling on foot and all its substitutes, all forms of transportation.

The poet, reckons Cixous, creates in motion, writes as s/he moves, moves as s/he writes. Creation, dreaming, movement and art are entwined.

> So perhaps dreaming and writing do have to do with traversing the forest, journeying through the world, using all the available means of transport, using your own body as a form of transport.

So, in the poetics of life, the unification, which is the very basis of magic, is symbolized in Peter Redgrove's art by the constant references to the stars and clouds and oceans of the upper world, and to the black, unknown, secret, intimate sensations, which are the inner-world/underworld experiences. Few poets have written so gloriously, for example, of stars, like Redgrove. I can think of Rainer Maria Rilke, who conjured up gorgeous, rich starscapes, especially in the *Duino Elegies*. And Will Shakespeare: in every play there is always that sense of the vast heavens wheeling overhead. This is from Redgrove's poem 'The Wheel':

> ...and the universe
> In me turns, the sails of stars
> Flapping and dripping radiance,
>
> The pricked sheets of constellations
> Through which we see total light... (Man, 92-93)

Rilke's stars are not mere 'backdrops' to stylish poesie, but are juicy, tangy, edible things. Redgrove, too, created juicy stars: isn't that amazing – *wet* stars, stars drenched in water? (See the extract from 'Living in Falmouth', Part IX, quoted above, about Orion). The Redgrove-poet washed his hair in starlight in 'To the Water-Psychiatrist' (Man, 25): 'Dare I wash my head again, with lightning I In the water, starlight in the source?' The wardrobe-lady too (in 'Six Odes') is full of stars:

> She wears the gown with the constellations slashed into its dark lining,
> She undresses out of the night sky, each night of the year a different sky...
> She has combed star-rays into a shaggy night-dress. (SP, 83).

Of course, stars are a natural manifestation of the Goddess, because the Goddess is Mother Night, called Nut in ancient Egyptian mythology. In the famous illustration from thousands of years ago, the Goddess Nut stretches above the Earth in a vaulting curve. In the poetics of Rilke, Shakespeare and Redgrove, stars are not only 'out there', in the black sky, they are also 'in here', in the inner night sky. The two places are the same.

Air too is a symbol or manifestation for Peter Redgrove of powerful outerness/ innerness (and the movements between inner and outer). Air is often what gives the body its 'skin orgasm', so one can't ignore air, and in many poems Redgrove writes of air, or the wind, which is another form of the great 'invisible' which is all around, ignored but always there. So Redgrove speaks of electricity pylons 'choiring in the wind' (in the poem 'Transactions' [Man, 50]) or, in the poem 'Air', Redgrove wrote of '[t]he air from the inside darkness' (Man, 110):

> Blowing breath at each other,
> The air from the inside darkness
> Palpitates with the heartbeats,
> And it is living air. It is
> An invisible quicksilver flowing
> Round your fingers as you touch.
> Its touch is very great,
>
> It is a diffused flesh, breathed from the warmth
> And the darkness inside which is not dark at all,
> Any more than the night of stars is dark,
> Black, without darkness.

If water is Peter Redgrove's first poetic element, air is his second, because air carries his primary non-visual sense, scent. Like the sea, the air too is infinite and eternally mobile. So in *A Crystal of Industrial Time*, Redgrove wrote of 'a perfumer's shop-cloud [which] surrounds me with its samples breaking over my shoulders' (CIT, 61). The imagery here recalls many of those in Patrick Süskind's novel *Perfume* (which Redgrove cited in *The Black Goddess and the Sixth Sense*, though there was a trendy European sadomasochism in *Perfume* which's out-of-sync with Redgrove's poetics of supersenses).[8]

Like Ted Hughes, Peter Redgrove is an immensely *elemental* poet, which is also how one might describe William Shakespeare, John

SEX–MAGIC–POETRY–CORNWALL

Cowper Powys and Sappho, because the elements are always raging through their work. In Redgrove's *œuvre*, all of these strands of experience are unified. So one cannot speak of water, for example, without also bringing in eroticism, women, storms, electricity, ecstasy, skin, alchemy, science, wombs, birth, etc. One of my favourite experiences in Redgrove's work of air and scent – and water and touch – is the opening of the poem 'Harvest', published in *The First Earthquake* (14), which fuses eroticism, touch, colour, symbolism, alchemy, perfume, the feminine, nature and synæsthesia:

> The greatest possible touch, to bathe.
> The wind bathing in the wheat,
> The great invisible woman plunges
> into the heavy tassels, into the wheat-smell
> That is like straw baskets full of new bread;
> The wheat splashes round her, it must cry out,
> All the stems chafing, like an immense piano plunged into
> Which continues playing as she swims...

You've got all the senses here, powerfully – and systematically, in the Rimbaudian sense – evoked (BG, 122f). Bathing in wheat – there's a glorious experience! And erotic too, but erotic in the expansive, cosmic sense, not in the limiting sense of genitals or porn. And alchemical too – the image recalls alchemical gold, and the red of blood/ passion/ energy/ life itself (it is an ovulation image, too, as described in *Alchemy For Women*). And also, this image of wheat recalls the final ecstasy and unifying vision of Wolf in John Cowper Powys's 1929 novel *Wolf Solent*, where the protagonist plunges his hands into the Byzantine gold, Cimmerian gold and Saturnian gold of a wheatfield.[9] Yet all this golden splendour comes from the black earth, and this is what Redgrove tries to nourish: the sense of rebirth from darkness, from what he calls 'the dark senses' or underworld. 'The dark world enriches the visible one' he wrote in 'His Upbringing' (Lab, 58).

3.5 Underworld / Underlife

Peter Redgrove created a mythopœia out of the 'dark senses' (BG, 94), which he termed *horasis*, carnal knowledge, *le rêve*, the sixth sense, Blake's Fifth Window, or *Daath*. The drive of Redgrove's argument in *The Black Goddess and the Sixth Sense* is this: that life is enriched when you actively engage with extra-sensuous perception. Redgrove drew on a tradition – that goes back to the Romantic poets primarily – of extra-sensuously perceptive poetry: Johann Wolfgang von Goethe, Novalis, Samuel Taylor Coleridge, William Wordsworth, Thomas Traherne, Arthur Rimbaud, Rainer Maria Rilke and St-John Perse (Redgrove cited most of those poets many times in his writings). In sex, the 'dark senses' means the touch of the lover's skin: 'to taste one's partner; and to meditate on your mutual incense; and to sink post-coitally into dream and out of it' (AFW, 129).

Like Aldous Huxley, who drew together many different strands of mysticism for his book *The Perennial Philosophy,* Peter Redgrove brought together many different types of extra-sensuous perception – including yoga, meditation, High Magic, daydreaming, weather-sensitivity and sleep. Carl Jung too had this kind of comprehensive or encyclopædical approach, which is found throughout his epic *Collected Works*. It annoys purists, though, who claim that you can't lump the absolutist monism of Sufism with the annihilation of Buddhism's *nirvana*, for example. For critics and purists, religious ecstasies don't mix, they are contextually-bound, and stem from and go towards different sources and goals.[1]

For religionists, theologians and mystics, it is abhorrent to confuse the Islamic dissolution of self in Allah with the Catholic union of self and God. In Sufic mystical ecstasy, there is no 'union', as if self and Allah were getting into bed with each other. There is simply oblivion, like the moth expiring in a candle flame, to use a famous analogy.[2] For Christians and Westerners, there is always something of the self, the ego, retained in the *unio mystica*.

SEX–MAGIC–POETRY–CORNWALL

Well, what Peter Redgrove did was to take the psychological approach of C.G. Jung, John Layard and natural science. That is, to study not the theological goals of ecstasy, or the socio-religious contexts, but the psycho-physical effects on the individual, on emotions and the body. That way, one can compare the ecstasies of Hinduism's *samadhi*, Zen Buddhism's *satori*, Sufism's bliss, Buddhism's *nirvana* or Buddhahood, daydreams, hypnagogia, trances, etc. Psychology broadens the fields of enquiry, and links together religion, magic, mythology, art, visions, poetry, theology, occultism, and so on. One is free to move about in all directions, because the focus is on the individual. Redgrove's mythopœia is founded on the individual, and is not part of establishment religion (although you might say that magic/ occultism/ hermeticism is a kind of establishment – now going through a new manifestation with the 'New Age' and 'Mind/ Body/ Spirit' phenomenon).

Redgrove's 'unknowing' or 'synæsthetic plenum of the unconscious or subliminal senses' (BG, 123) is found in all religions and mysticisms. To cater for all eventualities, Redgrove gave his pellucid apperception different names, linking it with Tantrism, Gnosticism (the Goddess Sophia), ritual magicke, yoga, alchemy, etc.

He called this extra-sensuous perception the Black Goddess, of which more later. It is the 'underlife' of John Cowper Powys, the underworld where Isis, Jesus, Orpheus and other heroes go. They travel to recover life itself, to be reborn. Orpheus goes to rescue Eurydice – his spirit familiar, his *anima*, his inspiration, his Muse, his Goddess, his alchemical counterpart (a journey most eloquently lyricized in modern times in Rainer Maria Rilke's great poem 'Orpheus. Eurydice. Hermes').

In the Redgrove multiverse, the fundamental journey is death and rebirth, symbolized every month by the menstrual cycle. Robert Graves related the death and rebirth of the poet to the ancient god or consort of the Goddess, who was ritually sacrificed on the Midsummer pyres and reborn as the Christ child or new king at the Winter Solstice or Christmas. This cycle of rebirth is what Graves called the Prime Theme or 'monomyth'.[3] Redgrove concurred with this death-rebirth journey, writing: 'goddess-worship means: transformation and rebirth' (BG, xxiv). And Redgrove's contemporary, Ted Hughes, has analyzed all of Shakespeare's work on the basis of Graves's monomyth (in his book *Shakespeare and the Goddess of Complete Being*).

The egg in menstruation dies and is reborn, like the poet, like the consort of the Goddess, like the woman herself, who is fragmented then reconstituted every moon, every month. The menstrual dimension was as important for Redgrove as alchemy or weather-sensitivity.

The nature of blackness in Redgrove's poetic cosmos is not that of William Shakespeare's Dark Lady, who was 'as black as hell' (sonnet 147.14). The Shakespeare-poet's one-time Muse was a Black Goddess, but of the ferocious, devouring kind, where women are seen as the 'gateway to hell', as Tertullian, Origen and other early Christian fathers asserted. Shakespeare's Dark Lady is partly fierce because she is the projection of the poet's anxieties concerning that highly-charged erotic entanglement between the poet, the fair youth and the woman.[4] (And the characters're all aspects of the Shakespeare-poet, too, and were never 'real people', nor meant to be; and they're simply figments of a poetic text, too, fictional characters to be manipulated by the poet. Yet the *Sonnets* are also Shakespeare at his most autobiographical and emotional).

In patriarchal religion, these concepts conjoin: death-women-vagina-hell-decay-sin-sex (the tradition of the Marquis de Sade, Charles Baudelaire, Georges Bataille and the Surrealists reduce it to the terms 'sex and death'. Odd, too, how so many of those writers and artists on sex and death are French). Redgrove's 'underworld' is similarly a feminine space, though purged of patriarchal hatred, for Redgrove has embraced the so-called 'dark side' of people and sexuality. Redgrove's is a thoroughly heterosexual vision of life, however, and his views could be seen, like those of Robert Graves, as sexist. As French feminists such as Hélène Cixous have shown, dualities such as masculine/ feminine or man/ woman are reductive; they limit life.

SEX–MAGIC–POETRY–CORNWALL

In Peter Redgrove's poetic world, black is associated with many of the usual things in occult philosophy: night, Mother Night, Black Goddess, Kali-Yuga (night in Indian mythology), the *yin* of Taoist mysticism, the superdazzling darkness of Catholicism (in St John of the Cross, *The Cloud of Unknowing*, Novalis, etc), witchcraft, prophecy, blood mysteries, alchemy, etc. Black is the state before regeneration in alchemy, the space before time in cosmology, the place of seeds and wombs. Blackness is supremely the Goddess's space, the 'moon-place' as Redgrove calls it, where creations occur. D.H. Lawrence often wrote of people as seeds buried in the soil, waiting to grow, as he described Will Brangwen in *The Rainbow*.[5]

Redgrove doesn't rate D.H. Lawrence highly as an influence, but this motif of the seed under the ground in soft, dark soil waiting to grow is archetypal Redgrove, really. Seeds appear in Redgrove's poem 'Lunar Mane', where all those storms and rainfalls beloved of Redgrove are associated clearly with the Goddess. In this poem, the Goddess appears as the controller of the weather, as the Goddess was in ancient times the creator of such powers:

> Low thunder and flashes of lightning
> emitted by her in lunar cycle; the rich clouds
> Pass over the full moon... (IHS,35)

The Goddess here is like the Chinese dragon, which brings storms and rain when it flies by. The dragon is a powerful embodiment of feminine mysteries (in both Eastern and Western magical traditions), and one sees dragonish alchemy seething throughout Redgrove's poetry (as the child sees the dragonish shapes in the womb in one of his poems).

What is clear by now is that there are more important things for Redgrove than magic, poetry, yoga, alchemy, landscape or weather-sensitivity, and that is the Goddess, or love, or women.

4

The Goddess and Feminism

> I am Nature, the Mother of all
> Mistress of the elements,
> Sovereign of the Spirit,
> Queen of the Dead,
> Queen of the Immortals,
> The single embodiment of all goddesses and gods
> ...I am Isis.
>
> Isis, in Apuleius' *Metamorphoses*[1]

4.1 The Return of the Goddess – Again

The Goddess (or spiritual femininity, or feminist spirituality) has been reappearing for poets, neo-pagans, New Agers, hippies, artists, writers, witches and magicians since the 1970s. 'There is no question in my mind that the Goddess is reawakening,' remarked Merlin Stone.[1] The Goddess is the alternative to the Judæo-Christian God, to the jealous, merciless Biblical Father-God, the tyrant of patriarchy, the old man

SEX–MAGIC–POETRY–CORNWALL

with the white beard who presides over the male mysteries of brotherhood, initiations and violence. The Goddess is the embodiment of feminine mysteries and female energy. She is politically green, ecologically sensitive, the Mother Earth figure, the mother of everyone, a reaction against greedy multinational conglomerates, against the military-industrial complex, against egotistical white Anglo-Saxon 'first world' Americanized globalized corporate capitalist materialist consumerist right-wing Imperialist urban-centred money-driven culture.

The Goddess (or female spirituality) became really popular with the rise of feminism and counter-culture in the 1960s. She was there before that – in the works of Robert Graves, J.J. Bachofen, Erich Neumann, C.G. Jung, J.G. Frazer, Robert Briffault and others. One can detect the presence of the Goddess in the art of William Shakespeare, Thomas Hardy, Rainer Maria Rilke, Sappho, Francesco Petrarch, the troubadours, all manner of mediæval poets, in the poets of ancient Egypt, Babylon, Sumer, India, China, and so on.

Historically, the Goddess is the powerful deity of the ancient and Classical era, with names like Isis, Ishtar, Demeter, Venus, Sophia, Venus, Kali, etc. Before the historic era, there was the rise of agriculture and that sacred identification of women-Earth-fertility-seasons, etc, embodied in those headless and nameless figurines of prehistoric times, the so-called stone "Venuses".

Mr Redgrove calls the Goddess the Genetrix, the Creatix, the Initiatrix, the Inspiratrix (a lot of 'trixes'), the Muse, the primal womb or vulva, the origin of all things; the Goddess's name in most cultures is derived from the word for womb or vagina, he claimed (WW, 169). Before the prehistoric era, no one knows just how far back Goddess worship goes, although, significantly, there is no father-figure in prehistory: 'there is no trace of a father figure in any of the Paleolithic periods. The life-creating power seems to have been of the Great Goddess alone', wrote Marija Gimbutas (316). No father figure! This is a blow to followers of Freud, Lacan, Hamlet and Oedipus!

For Goddess poets such as Peter Redgrove and Robert Graves, the

SEX–MAGIC–POETRY–CORNWALL

Goddess was usurped by male power in the Classical age, and male deities were set up in her stead: Apollo, Dionysus, Jesus and Jehovah. For Redgrove and Chris Knight, men took over women's mysteries – the blood mysteries of menstruation, sexuality and childbirth. For Redgrove and Knight, men stole women's power, creating a patriarchal state of law, and the basis of the struggle was in the powergaming centred on sex.[2] Employing the methods that have become familiar – violence, force, coercion, persuasion, propaganda and dogma – men (or more accurately, masculine society) took social and emotional power away from women. The patriarchal quality of Western culture since that time has been determined by this white noise of disinformation concerning sexuality, menstruation, conception, pregnancy, child rearing, education, the family and work.

The resurgence of the Goddess, then, is the religious or spiritual dimension, you might say, of feminism. The Goddess is a new spiritual development centred on an ancient spiritual feeling, a way of living that is dynamic and empowering, healing and nurturing. There are many books on the Goddess around now – by Elinor Gadon, Monica Sjöo, Caitlin Matthews, Barbara Walker, Esther Harding, Marina Warner, Shirley Nicholson, etc. And many artists who use the Goddess in their images and sculptures: Judy Chicago, Ana Mendieta, Niki Sant-Phalle, Miriam Schapiro, Mary Beth Edelson, Louise Bourgeois and Meinrad Craighead. Judy Chicago said her aim was 'to make the feminine holy'.[3] Goddess philosophy is about holism, healing, energizing, visioning, empathy, earthing, weaving, nurturance, compassion, union, emotion – there is a new language being created to cater for the anti-patriarchal nature of the Goddess cult.[4]

The Goddess movement is a small but powerful part of Western culture – linked with contemporary phenomena such as the rise of witchcraft (again), UFOlogy, Tarot, astrology, earth magic, shamanism, ley lines, all kinds of 'occultism', while on the other side, Goddess worship is centred in radical feminism, in the marvellous work of feminists such as Mary Daly and Barbara G. Walker.

SEX–MAGIC–POETRY–CORNWALL

Peter Redgrove was part of that resurgence of Goddess culture – worship isn't too strong a word. For him, it was partly all about cunt. As he (and Shuttle) wrote in *The Wise Wound*, 'the Queen is *cwen*, or wife with the *quim*, which is a *combe* or *cwm*, the *gune* (woman) is a goddess when she is *gana* and *jani* (woman) with a *yoni*, or cunt' (WW, 169).

These are exciting times, fantastic times, for women and feminism. There are some magnificent feminist writers about: Andrea Dworkin, for instance, who was a one-woman revolution, the most incisive polemicist of our time, as her books show (*Pornography*, 1981, and *Intercourse*, 1987, for example). Or Elizabeth Grosz, an intelligent, subtle and incisive feminist critic. There are the French feminists (who disagree with the Anglo-American feminists at many points in their readings of patriarchal culture), but who nevertheless call for women to break into wild creativity and passion: Hélène Cixous, Luce Irigaray, Julia Kristeva, Xavière Gauthier and Monique Wittig.

What has all this to do with Peter Redgrove? Everything, in fact. Redgrove – and Penelope Shuttle – work within this Goddess and feminist tradition. Their book *The Wise Wound* was an important contribution to understanding the magico-religious aspects of women's sexuality (and *Alchemy For Women* further developed their argument). Redgrove's poetry comes from the Goddess experience, the 'mother-world', and all his poems can be seen as Goddess poems: from the obvious menstrual eulogy of 'Starlight' to the dragon-wild storm-bringing of 'Rainmaking Exercise' and 'The Pale Brows of Lightning'.

Redgrove exalts women's power. In the poem 'The Grand Lunacy' he writes of the Moon as 'the mansion of the mighty mother' (WNP, 43); in *In the Country of the Skin* the Black Goddess, Teresa, is 'the black lover of animals' (33); while in 'An Egyptian Requiem', Redgrove makes the age-old connection between women, life/ death, the Moon, night, stars and transformation:

SEX–MAGIC–POETRY–CORNWALL

Beyond the Hall

Where you eat your heart, is a garden
Which still exists, though men deny it.
This is the starting-point.

As when the Moon dies, and her bones whiten
And crumble into dust of stars, the nightside
Of phenomena where all transforms. (Man, 39)

And in 'The Goging Stool', from *The Mudlark Poems*, he writes:

The HWCH or Witch. The scribe, the scraper,
The spirit-sculptor of the Mother of All,
Mother of Source, the Widow, the One Alone,
Communicator. All that belonged to that firstness
Was afterwards derided and denounced but is. (Mud, 19)

Redgrove's particular Goddess is Black, called variously Hecate, Isis, Persephone, Medusa, Lilith, Sophia, Kore and Mary Magdalene (BG, xxiii).[5] It is this 'invisible' Goddess that Redgrove enshrines in his poetry: '[t]he greatest art depicts these invisibles, the bounty of the goddess', he asserts (BG, 69).

Peter Redgrove developed his Black Goddess from Robert Graves, who said she 'represents... a miraculous certitude in love'.[6] Graves never created a systematic mythology of poetry of the Black Goddess, as he did of the White Goddess. He wrote a book on the Black Goddess, but never worked up this hidden, invisible side of his Goddess into something as full-blown as the material in *The White Goddess*.

Robert Graves's black mysticism of love is truly ecstatic, for it always emphasizes timelessness, transcendence, bliss and union, speaking of a 'timeless now'.[7] Redgrove is as ecstatic as Graves' late work, at times. Like Graves, Redgrove believes passionately in the Gnostic/ Neoplatonic ideality of love, where two souls can be 'unalterably one' as Graves put it in a poem. Redgrove said:

the things that women can give on the personal level by their companionship, their motherhood, and their sexuality are so close to the things that I want to say in poetry. All of my poetry in that sense is love poetry. I'm looking for the missing half, if you like, of the Platonic body, trying to find this in my poetry. (PR, 7)

So Redgrove searched for his other half, the 'secret sharer', the other soul in the gnostic *syzygy*, that egg which contains two souls like two yolks, the double pelican of alchemy, where two beings initiate and feed each other. This is one of the most deeply desired dreams of Western culture, this two-in-oneness, this mystical union or spiritual marriage, where the King and Queen, brother and sister, sun and moon of alchemy join together.

For the historical origin of this powerful desire for love-union we go back to that mythic figure who, like Orpheus, stands behind so much of Western magic and religion, Plato. In his *Symposium*, Plato wrote:

Each of us when separated is always looking for his other half; such a nature is prone to love and ready to return love. And when he finds his other half, the pair are lost in an amazement of love and friendship and intimacy.[8]

This dream of love lies behind any number of works of art from the last two millennia: Francesco Petrarch's *Canzoniere*, William Shakespeare's *Sonnets*, Thomas Hardy's novels and poetry, Dante Alighieri's *Vita Nuova*, John Donne's *Songs*, Johann Wolfgang von Goethe's *Werther* or André Gide's *Strait Is the Gate*. In the apocryphal *Gospel of Thomas* Jesus says

When you make the two one, and when you make the inner as the outer and the outer as the inner and the above as the below... then shall you enter the Kingdom.[9]

Here, Jesus restates the central tenet of Western magic: *as above, so below*, which can also be translated as: *as outside, so inside*.

In *The Black Goddess and the Sixth Sense*, Redgrove wrote

SEX–MAGIC–POETRY–CORNWALL

> [the Black Goddess is] the world's hope-in-love... the symbol and gateway to everything we could know in the apparent blackness beyond visible sight... [she is] the goddess of clairvoyance, clear-seeing and second sight... the lover's light of touch in bed, and the dark night of touch in the womb. She is the Goddess of Intimacy, of being 'in touch' and of that fifth window, the skin...(136-7)

The figure of the Goddess plays a key role in this unification of love. As Peter Redgrove says, he is more interested in Shakespeare's sister than the old bard himself.[10] There are many antecedents of the Black Goddess: Sophia, the Gnostic Goddess of Wisdom; the 'black but comely' Shulamite of the *Song of Songs*; the Black Madonna statues found throughout Europe; Lilith, Adam's first lover; Isis; Diana, the Goddess of witches; the Night Mare or succubus; Kali, the Indian Goddess; Hecate; Persephone; Shekinah of Qabbalism; and the Sphinx. Black Goddesses are found in Egyptian religion, Catharism, Arthurian and Grail romances, alchemy, Neoplatonism, witchcraft and the Knights Templar.

There is maybe an element of racism, for detractors, in all this talk of 'blackness'. Mr Redgrove is not racist, but images of race occur in his texts, such as the black man in his novel *The God of Glass*. Here, though, the blackness does not refer to ethnic origins but to magic, the unconscious and the 'underlife' of things. Redgrove relates the Black Goddess to the original Mother of All, the woman who gave birth to everyone, who lived in Africa thousands of years ago.[11]

This talk of blood ties and blackness can appear dubious, ideologically. Indeed, Bertrand Russell says that any talk of blood and hereditary relations is automatically racist and right-wing.[12] Redgrove's own politics move towards liberalism and the left. The racism, rather, is built into the language. Words such as 'black' or 'blackness' cannot be used without some critics drawing attention to their ideological connotations. But, as the feminist Julia Kristeva noted, meaning is contextual, and in the context of Redgrove's poetry, 'blackness' is magical not political.

4.2 Feminism

Peter Redgrove and Penelope Shuttle wrote in *The Hermaphrodite Album* that '[d]arkness is a power. She haunts with power' (from the poem 'Erosion' [67]). *The Hermaphrodite Album* was a collaboration, the title of which again refers to the longed-for alchemical, mystic union. By speaking of the Goddess, Shuttle and Redgrove hoped to redefine heterosexual relations. The Goddess was seen as a timely counterblast to patriarchy, to 'the strictures of over-masculinized society' as Shuttle puts it (We, 125).

Redgrove employed some of the notions of the French feminists (Hélène Cixous, Luce Irigaray, Xavière Gauthier and Julia Kristeva), which in turn were derived in part from (or opposed to) the 'French Freud', Jacques Lacan. Redgrove used the notion of *jouissance*, for example, the orgasmic nature of writing and texts and reading, a favourite term of Lacan's and Cixous'. Or the 'hysterization of the skin' (Rim, 174). French feminists such as Julia Kristeva celebrated female eroticism, speaking in *About Chinese Women* of the 'explosive, blossoming, sane and inexhaustible *jouissance* of the woman'.[1]

It was Luce Irigaray who wrote of all-over female eroticism, saying 'women has sex organs just about everywhere'.[2] For Irigaray, a woman's sex (her vulva) is 'two lips which embrace continually'.[3] (Irigaray's emphasis on the labia ignores the clitoris, the vagina, and the womb. Clitoral lovemaking, like menstrual sex, is part of Redgrove's poetry).

Some feminists have disagreed with Luce Irigaray's biologist-based statement about labia, because it over-emphasizes eroticism, at the expense of other aspects. This may be Redgrove's problem too: that, in stressing sexuality, feminists limit their notion of what women are. By reducing people to erotic creatures they limit their potential, as Sigmund Freud did by sexualizing everything. In the Freudian view (which is also that of the Marquis de Sade, Charles Baudelaire, Georges Bataille and others), the whole world is erotic – caves are vaginas, towers are phalloi. For the intellectuals, sex and death combine, and everything is reducible to sex and death, every drive relates to the sex drive ('birth, copulation and death', said T.S. Eliot, summarizing the cynical, oh-so-clever masculinist view). All this is severely reductive, squashing the life out of life.

Peter Redgrove at times seems to go along with feminists in preaching the sexual superiority of women, of the clitoris, the super-sensitivity of women, and the multi-orgasmic capabilities of women (he is not much concerned with the old argument of clitoral vs. vaginal orgasm. The clitoris isn't cited in his poetry as much as the vulva and its elixir ('cunt dew'), but there are a few references. In the poem 'The Dark Bell' Redgrove remarks: 'she was well-clitorised for the fourth time that Sunday' [FVC, 62]). Both Redgrove and Shuttle regarded the clitoris as superior to the penis when it came to sensuous experience (WW, 32).

The trouble with comparing male and female sensuality is that women's sensuality is always defined *in opposition to* – and in relation to – men's sensuality. Hélène Cixous showed how limiting it is to speak in terms of 'woman' and 'man'.[4] Cixous' Derridean analysis revealed how duality upholds the patriarchal status quo. By stressing the sexual superiority of women, feminists acknowledged male sexuality as the only alternative, as the 'guide' by which to judge female sexuality. They uphold the sexual stereotypes. Instead of men and women, we get reductions to the clitoris and penis. And sex – and people – are more than that. Sex is more than the rubbing together of penis and clitoris. It might be far better to speak of *difference*, as Monique Wittig, Luce Irigaray and Bonnie Zimmerman suggest (but not just gender differences, but differences between individuals. Besides, the gender difference issue has been over-done in feminist, gay and queer criticism, and there are infinitely more similarities than differences between men and women and their sexualities.)[5]

The emphasis on sexual issues can obscure other crucial issues: of ethnicity, of power relations, of enculturation, of labour, of class, of ideology, of agency, etc. In Peter Redgrove's poesie, there's a lot of sex, and a lot of genitals. For example: 'her cunt gave off a round heat that was in itself a dream.' (CIT, 59) Redgrove focuses on sexuality, because for him being alive is itself erotic: his relation with the world is erotic, just as his poems can be seen as 'acts of love'.[6]

Redgrove advocated a multilayered relation to life, hating the reductionist view that sees women as mere 'cunt', where their only function is to be fucked. As Elizabeth Carola wrote: 'the basic male fantasy of Woman as Wholly Sexual Object whose Purpose is To Be Fucked'.[7] Andrea Dworkin in her astonishing book *Pornography* summ-arizes the patriarchal view neatly:

> Commonly referred to as 'it,' sex is defined in action only by what the male does with his penis. Fucking – the penis thrusting – is the magical, hidden meaning of "it," the reason for sex... In the male system, sex is the penis, the penis is sexual power, its use in fucking is manhood.[8]

Dworkin's polemic is powerful, and is one area of feminism. She makes sweeping generalizations, that derive from a deep-seated rage. Her radical feminism can be applied to many aspects of the global media landscape (though Dworkin's views are still controversial, and not accepted by many feminists). Redgrove himself is somewhere in the middle ground, somewhere between eroticism and poetry. He said:

> I tend to fall between two stools. I become unpopular with feminists and slightly unpopular with masculinists. I think I may write prim-arily for women of intelligence and sexuality, who know sexuality is funny as well as spiritual. (Laz)

Sometimes Redgrove's texts employ dualist terms and gender stereotypes, but his intentions are *not* to be stereotypical. Redgrove exalts women, and that, he says, can be seen as sexist. In masculine two-term logocentrism, the male binary logic of the West, life is reduced to male and female, and even further, to penis and vagina, and we know which is regarded as superior. Everywhere is this 'us and them' philosophy found at work – in racism, sexism, ageism, classism, nationalism.

French feminists were wary of using terms such as 'woman', 'feminine' and 'women'. For example, Alice Jardine said that the term 'woman' is really a 'writing-effect'.[9] The problem is that language, our whole reference-system, is thoroughly patriarchal. Or is it? Feminists debate this issue hotly, because language is at the heart of feminism, and touches so many crucial aspects of life. Dale Spender called language 'man-made',[10] while Hélène Cixous hated the term 'feminine'.[11] Mary Daly tried to counter patriarchal language by creating one of her own, as has Barbara G. Walker (either by coining new words, or by reclaiming existing words and giving them new meanings. This aspect of second wave feminism threw up some fascinating new languages – have a look at the feminist dictionaries and handbooks from the 1980s, for instance).[12]

In French feminism the text is primary, and a text can be 'feminine' regardless of who wrote it. A man can write a 'feminine' text (such as Jean Genet). However, according to Hélène Cixous, there are only one or two truly 'feminine' texts (she mentions Colette, Marguerite Duras and Genet). Redgrove's poetry is thoroughly feminized, however, rejoicing in the pleasure (*jouissance*) of the text.

Feminists bite back against patriarchal culture and society, and there is so much to attack and redress. Peter Redgrove and Penny Shuttle have done their bit by writing *The Wise Wound* and *Alchemy For Women*, which have helped to uncover the taboo-driven disinformation that men have heaped upon menstruation and women's mysteries.

'We're stormy,' says Hélène Cixous,[13] and feminists reckon that women are much wilder and stranger than men. Not 'wilder and stranger' in themselves, but women's *cultural space* is wilder and stranger. The *female* 'wild zone', to use Elaine Showalter's useful term, is much wilder and stranger than the *male* 'wild zone'. We know about the male 'wild zone' – it's the stuff of legend, of hunting, of violence, wars, brotherhoods, initiations, etc.[14] The female 'wild zone' is that moon-place/ womb-space of menstrual madness, blood mysteries and women's adventures. The 'wild zone' is a cultural, not a biological space; that is, things experienced there are beyond established male *culture*, and a new language has to be invented to describe experiences in the female 'wild zone'.

Biologist or essentialist arguments are regarded with suspicion by many feminists (especially third wave or postmodern feminists). This is the key point of French feminism: that women are not born, one *becomes* a woman, as Simone de Beauvoir put it (E. Marks, 152). Or as Sheila Jeffreys wrote: '[e]very woman grows up in a heteropatriarchal world'.[15] Women can re-possess their bodies physically (though even that can be difficult), but *culturally* the task is problematic.

Body-awareness is crucial. French feminists such as Madeleine Gagnon write that '[a]ll we have to do is let the body flow, from the inside' (E. Marks, 180). You'll see the body flowing throughout Redgrove's poems.

The biologist/ essentialist analysis is not the whole picture, though, and third wave and postmodern feminism has been very critical of second wave feminism's emphasis on the body, on biology, of reducing women to biological essences (including sexual essences). Redgrove's sexual politics were formed in the 1960s and 1970s, in the 'permissive' era of 'women's liberation', the age of the Pill and 'free love'. Those hippy ideals (Redgrove is unashamedly a hippy) have been criticized in the age of AIDS and postmodernism (Redgrove's æsthetics are modernist). On the one hand, the New Right, the religious right in the US, and the liberal political correctness lobbies have frowned upon the promiscuity and hedonism of the Sixties and Seventies, which can't be sustained in the era of AIDS. The new puritanism is suspicious of anything pleasurable. At the same time, the depictions of explicit sexuality in pornography have become mainstream, and the porn industry is endlessly examined in TV documentaries and the popular media. Porn, sex and decadence are no big deal anymore, but on the other hand, censorship and repression is tighter than ever. There's more repression around – political, social, legal *and* cultural – than for many decades.

SEX–MAGIC–POETRY–CORNWALL

Peter Redgrove and Penelope Shuttle, in *The Wise Wound*, used ancient myths in their analysis of menstrual taboos, which may cause problems, because most of the myths were made by and for men. So the Goddess of Classical times may be a male construct. Even if the authors were not mostly male – and they surely were – the *texts themselves* are patriarchal, and it is on the texts that we base much of our knowledge about those times and people.

Shuttle's and Redgrove's goal was to investigate the taboos that have grown up around menstruation, and to use the ancient mythologies as corroborative illustrations of their thesis. Although patriarchy is embedded so deeply in language and culture, it may be possible to extract an 'authentic' 'feminine' view from them. The 'feminine' is there, for those who can see it and Shuttle and Redgrove saw it. For some feminists, there is something in women way beyond men's grasp. As Xavière Gauthier wrote:

> ...witches [women] are bursting; their entire bodies are desire; their gestures are caresses; their smell, taste, hearing are all sensual. Their pleasure is so violent, so transgressive, so open, so fatal, that men have not yet recovered. (E. Marks, 201)

One might say that Redgrove's work is an attempt to set in writing some of his experiences of this violent, transgressive, multi-sensual and open *jouissance*.

Redgrove adores women, but that very adoration can have sexist implications. Goddess worship, for instance, is sexist, defining gender roles and setting out power relations clearly. Goddess worship says men will act like this, and women like that, and, further, it is usually ruthlessly heterosexual (as are witchcraft covens with their six men, six women and presiding priest/ess – witchcraft and pagan rituals, which emphasize heterosexual relations all the way down the line, can be as sexist and stereotypical as Christianity).[16]

There's a 'Duchess of Cunt' in the poem 'From Love's Journeys' (Dr, 65), which some feminists would interpret negatively ('the | Duchess of

Cunt was waiting | to award me my | school prize of sex- | instruction booklets'). If there is sexism and anti-feminism in Peter Redgrove's works, it's part of just about *all texts everywhere.* A good deal of *The Wise Wound* is given over to a history of how women have been oppressed – in the mass murder of the witches in the Middle Ages which Shuttle and Redgrove call 'nine million menstrual murders'. *The Wise Wound*, Redgrove said, is about

> the way the masculine non-menstruating spirit prevents women from achieving their own visionary riches by shutting them into a hell of disinformation and stealing the one half of their sexuality – the tabooed menstrual half. (Rim, 174)

Shuttle and Redgrove's menstrual book is dedicated to the creation of a menstrual zone, a female 'wild zone'. So feminists speak of experiences beyond male control: pregnancy, childbirth, female orgasm, *jouissance*. Julia Kristeva wrote:

> If a woman cannot be part of the temporal symbolic order except by identifying with the father, it is clear that as soon as she shows any sign of that which, in herself, escapes such identification and acts differently, resembling the dream of the maternal body, she evolves into this 'truth' in question. It is thus that female specificity defines itself in patrilinear society: woman is a specialist in the unconscious, a witch, a bacchanalian, taking her *jouissance* in an anti-Apollonian, Dionysian orgy.[17]

Like the poet, 'woman' is a shaman, a witch, a magician, moving beyond the symbolic/ oedipal/ patriarchal order. Redgrove concurs with this view of 'woman' as witch, shaman, Goddess: he has any number of witchy poems: 'At the Witch Museum', 'Room of Wax', 'Young Women With the Hair of Witches and No Modesty' and 'The Wicked One'. In 'Water-Witch, Wood-Witch, Wine-Witch', he writes about making love in a cornfield (Dr,11), an image of maximum fertility:

SEX–MAGIC–POETRY–CORNWALL

> She uncaps jars of venomous honey. I take her by the hips
> And lift her down as from a tree. In the cornfield we make our
>   love
> And as we finish the air is thickly grassed with rain.
>   Who was it
> Who smelt even as she frowned in anger
> Of blueberries and honey, in whose honour
> Corn-lightning played over the horizon?

For Redgrove, a witch is a woman in tune with her menstrual cycle. Society, he says, elevates the ovulatory aspect of things – the mother, the passive nurturer (the Virgin Mary is the archetype) – but denigrates and denies the menstrual woman, the witch, the 'witchy' woman who becomes objectified as a whore, because she uses transformative, non-procreative sex (i.e., sex during menstruation). The virgin/ whore or mother/ lover or ovulation/ menstruation duality is found throughout Western culture – in the Virgin Mary/ Mary Magdalene, or in Eve/ Lilith, or in the two aspects of Aphrodite.[18]

Peter Redgrove's Goddess has a cosmic dimension. She becomes identified with the fundamental processes of life itself, she is space and time, says Joseph Campbell, while Erich Neumann depicts her as the 'Great Round' into which everyone goes at death.[19] One is reminded of European tumuli and prehistoric tombs where bones were reddened with ochre at burial, perhaps relating to menstrual blood, but certainly relating to the blood of life.[20] There are many prehistoric sites in Cornwall, Redgrove's home county, particularly in the West Penwith peninsula, and this aspect of the Cornish landscape – the massive sepulchral nature of the stones and the granite – finds its way into Redgrove's work (the stone circles are wonderful – Merry Maidens, Tregeseal, and the great Boscawen-Ûn, while the *fogous* or underground tunnels are superbly uterine and Redgrovean).

Curled up in the foetal position, death becomes a rebirth in a different kind of womb, a stone womb. Poets have long made the links between womb and tomb, which is another manifestation of the masculine association of sex and death. In Redgrove's poetics, the menstruating woman is the most powerful living being, and makes clear the mythopœic continuum of sex, death, rebirth and transformation. The film director Michelangelo Antonioni (of *Blow Up* fame) said that being with women makes life richer and deeper somehow: 'I especially love women... Through the psychology of women everything becomes more poignant'.[21] Redgrove writes, in the poem 'Among the Whips and the Mud Baths': '[h]er power makes me see things, I mean her personality' (SP,137), while in 'A Word' he muses:

> Women offer mastery
> Of night... (Man, 89)

For Redgrove, the best thing men can do is to live in mythopoetico-synæsthetic and multi-sensual relationship with women. Men must live with women, he says in his poetry and in his non-fiction.

4.3   Peter Redgrove and Julia Kristeva

Julia Kristeva has created a psychopoetry of the semiotic and the *chora*, a maternal realm which relates in many respects to Peter Redgrove's notion of 'mother-world'. The semiotic theories refer to the archaic maternal spaces or modalities which help to create art and poetry. It's worth looking at Kristeva's notion of the semiotic modality and the *chora*, for it bears trenchantly on Redgrove's poetics, and on the poetic quest. Kristeva breaks with Sigmund Freud and Jacques Lacan in her *chora* thesis: for she founds her philosophy of the *chora* not on the primacy of the phallus as 'transcendent signifier', as in the Lacanian system. Instead, there is a sublimation of maternal *jouissance*:

SEX–MAGIC–POETRY–CORNWALL

At that point we witness the possibility of creation, of sublimation. I think that every type of creation, even if it's scientific, is due to this possibility of opening the norms, towards pleasure, which refers to an archaic experience with a maternal pre-object. ("A Question of Subjectivity", 131)

From the *chora* and semiotic, then, flows poetry. This is where things get very interesting. Artistic creation becomes a struggle involving signification, transgression, the semiotic and the symbolic.

And so, according to psychoanalysis [writes Kristeva], poets as individuals fall under the category of fetishism; the very practice of art necessitates reinvesting the maternal *chora* so that it transgresses the symbolic order... the poetic function therefore converges with fetishism; it is not, however, identical to it. What distinguishes the poetic function from the fetishist mechanism is that it maintains a *signification* (*Bedeutung*). All its paths into, indeed valorizations of, pre-symbolic semiotic stases not only require the ensured maintenance of this signification but also serve signification, even when they dislocate it. No text, no matter how 'musicalized', is devoid of meaning or signification; on the contrary, musicalization pluralizes meanings. We may say therefore that the text is not a fetish. (*Desire In Language*, 115-6)

The poetic zone that Redgrove and other poets speak of or strive for is similar to Julia Kristeva's notion of the dark, pre-oedipal space of the mother, the *chora*. Michael Payne defined Kristeva's *chora* thus: 'a nourishing and maternal, pre-verbal semiotic space or state in which the linguistic sign has not yet been articulated as the absence of an object' (239). Redgrove's poetic alchemy relates to the maternal body as an actuality. As Kristeva wrote in *Desire in Language*: '[c]ells fuse, split, and proliferate; volumes grow, tissues stretch, and body fluids change rhythm, speeding up or slowing down. Within the body, growing as a graft, indomitable, there is an other' (237).

The 'other' is the child; the poet in Redgrove's work is pregnant with a different sort of child: her/ his art, the poem, the artwork as the Magical Child of alchemy. In *Revolution as Poetic Language*, Kristeva spoke of the *chora* as the place where 'the subject is both generated and negated' (28); it is 'a place of change, it is fluid, amorphous, 'pre-word', and, like a cell, divisible' (ib., 239-240n.). Language, though, can never circumscribe this maternal space: to name it is to change it.

In *Desire in Language,* Kristeva remarked:

> Poetic language, the only language that uses up transcendence and theology to sustain itself; poetic language, knowingly the enemy of religion, by its very economy borders on psychosis (as for its subject) and totalitarianism or fascism (as for the institution it implies or evokes). (125)

This can apply to Peter Redgrove's work (Kristeva thinks of Antonin Artaud, Vladimir Mayakovsky and Louis-Ferdinand Céline). Kristeva continued:

> Since at least Hölderlin, poetic language has deserted beauty and meaning to become a laboratory where, facing philosophy, knowledge, and the transcendental ego of all signification, the impossibility of a signified or signifying identity is being sustained. If we took this venture seriously – if we could hear the burst of black laughter it hurls at all attempts to master the human situation, to master language by language – we would be forced to re-examine "literary history', to rediscover beneath rhetoric and poetics its unchanging but always different polemic with the symbolic function. (*Desire in Language*, 145)

The poetic moment, for Kristeva, is founded on desire: desire is what keeps the system together:

> The other that will guide you and itself through this dissolution is a rhythm, music, and within language, a text. But what is the connection that holds you both together? Counter-desire, the negative of desire, inside-out desire, capable of questioning (or provoking) its own infinite quest. Romantic, filial, adolescent, exclusive, blind and Oedipal: it is all that, but for others. It returns to where you are, both of you, disappointed, irritated, ambitious, in love with history, critical, on the edge and even in the midst of its own identity crisis.

SEX–MAGIC–POETRY–CORNWALL

(*Desire In Language*, 165)

Sometimes Redgrove sometimes evokes sexuality in a similar way to the European intellectual tradition of Georges Bataille and Charles Baudelaire. The sexualization of the world can be found throughout his work. But the exploration of the 'mother-world', and women's mysteries such as menstruation, set Redgrove apart from the masculinist literary movement of the 20th century.

5

Sex Magic, Sex Alchemy, Sex Yoga

5.1   Menstrual Sex

When the woman is menstruating, lovemaking can be visionary and extraordinary, claimed Peter Redgrove. This is what everyone's interested in, he asserted: 'that is, a kind of sexuality which is transformative and not for reproduction'.[1] This transformative sex is hated by the church and tabooed by society, even as elements of society are fascinated by it. Witches cultivate the energies released during menstruation, says Redgrove, and he creates a magic, an alchemy, a yoga, a religion out of sex. 'The flower of yoga is, however, the sexual act', Redgrove asserted (AFW, 128).

For Redgrove, magic itself is erotic – 'true magic is a turn-on' (Rim, 175) – and poetry is erotic, and the erotic is poetic. 'The mutual illumination sex brings us is of a poetic nature' commented Penelope Shuttle (We, 127). Sex-poetry-magic-alchemy-yoga-Goddess-feminism-menstruation thus form a continuum which was central to Shuttle and Redgrove's life. Everything feeds into everything else. So the orgasmic state becomes creative, and one can ask 'it' things and maybe get back answers, or direct the reverie (like petitioning the unconscious mind during during dreaming). Shuttle explained thus:

> That 'continuity with nature' is what I mean by 'greening the orgasm' and can only be adequately described in poetry... Sex in which my orgasmic potential has been realized, taking Peter with me to match the female capacity, becomes timeless, egoless, and natural. (We, 131)

The post-orgasmic state was special, and sensitive, and should be closely guarded, Redgrove said: '[a]ll visions, dreams and fantasies occurring sexually should be treasured, recorded and expressed' (AFW, 133). Communing with the orgasmic state was

> like a prayer. Speak into the mystery, and the mystery answers. Questions or requests made in this trance-state will receive answers, either by a show of imagery, or by a thought coming into one's mind much later. (AFW, 138-9)

Redgrove advocated a sexual alchemy based on Tantric, Taoist and Oriental sexual magic, where the man withholds ejaculation and climbs the 'ladder' or 'staircase' of orgasms with the woman, who is multi-orgasmic. The man stays his orgasm at each of the orgasmic plateaus the woman experiences: she comes, he waits. When they reach the top of the 'ladder of orgasms', they come together.

Orgasm for the man wasn't the same as ejaculation, though: in Hatha yoga and Taoist yoga, male ejaculation can be withheld, so that the man experiences mini-climaxes with the woman (AFW, 138). Around four peaks were recommended in traditional sex manuals of the East, Redgrove said, not including a clitoral orgasm, with the lovers orgasming together at the end (AFW, 137).

In 'My Dog Barked Back', Redgrove wrote:

SEX–MAGIC–POETRY–CORNWALL

> To fuck, to enspirit, to pass the ghost,
> Riding through the bed in the meditation chariot;
> The goddess awoke to find herself a goddess,
> Singing her own song, and all the footman
> Clung together in fear,
>
> The tongue wallowing in its song-cave
> Was at the same time celestial music,
> Red dragon swimming the inner sea. (OE, 54)

There are good and bad days for sex in Redgrove and Shuttle's system, and one should use the good days or 'orgasmic windows' (We, 137). The aim is creative union: '[l]ove-making often leads to a creative clarity' he said (ib., 139). Redgrove wanted everyone to creatively dream (PV).

Masturbation was good, too, because sex in general was transformative for Redgrove, a way of moving through thresholds, a way of tuning the individual in to the universe, to life, to change. Redgrove wrote:

> Self-stimulation to orgasm is a great, a good way, as sex with a partner is, of disassembling oneself, as it were, and reconstituting on the other side of a threshold. It is thus the key to transformation. (*Alchemy For Women*, 59)

Orgasm was a way of balancing the body for Redgrove, and could help with PMS, POS, and dysmenorrhoea (AFW, 131).

It wasn't lovemaking as mere sexual sensation, though: 'orgasmic feeling is 'erotic' feeling,' Redgrove maintained, 'as opposed to sexual sensation'. It wasn't superficial, shallow sex. The whole purpose of this kind of sex was to turn ordinary life into erotic life, which might be the best way to be:

> to transform sexual sensation into erotic living. Erotic living is like the most passionate creative feeling coupled with a profound relaxation and openness. Perhaps it is our natural state. (AFW, 141)

SEX–MAGIC–POETRY–CORNWALL

And in *The Wise Wound*, Shuttle and Redgrove defined erotic living as a merging of mind and body in felt experience, a heightened and more meaningful perception of the world, so that sex results in 'a complex act of sensuous relationship to people and things in the outer world' (WW, 83).

In Redgrove's system, one chooses the right days in the menstrual cycle: when the egg dies, the potential child is sacrificed (as is the woman), and energy is released and produces transformation and spiritual renewal (ib., 140). This death-and-rebirth cycle is the biological dimension of the Goddess's consort dying and being reborn. The menstrual journey is thus a descent and return, and when the spiritual resurgence occurs, Redgrove said

> it is accompanied with an especial sexual high, which is alchemical and transforms the perceptions, so that everything that falsely appeared dull and 'ordinary' is transformed to the extraordinary, and makes poems that testify to the joy and the strangeness of descent and return... (We, 140)

You'll see this strangeness and joy in many poems: in 'Four Poems of Love and Transition', 'Starlight', 'Entry Fee' and 'A Maze Like Us', for example. These are orgasmic poems, created out of the orgasmic state. Sometimes Redgrove depicted his beloved as a human figure, but just as frequent are the orgasmic qualities of the natural elements – drenching storms, snaky zigzag lightning bolts, or the perfume rising off a lawn before rain (in 'Word' [Man, 89, and WI, 4]).

In the *Theatricum Chemicum*, an alchemical treatise, Gerhard Dorn wrote: '[t]ransform yourselves into living philosophical stones!' (quoted by C.G. Jung).[2] And this is precisely what the Redgrove-poet tries to do, to transform himself into a living Philosopher's Stone, to become the Holy Grail, the King-Queen alchemical unity. The Redgrove-poet gives himself wholly over to the woman, the Goddess. The amazing alchemist Paracelsus (d. 1541) wrote: 'he who would enter the kingdom of God must first enter with his body into his mother and there die'.[3]

Peter Redgrove, like Paracelsus, Cornelius Agrippa and the mediæval alchemists, advocated a 'dying to' the Goddess, much as Catholic mystics speak of 'dying to' Christ or God. Redgrove proposes a renaissance of the Goddess symbolized by what he calls an entry into the 'mother-world'. As Paracelsus says, rebirth is essential, but it requires a sacrifice, and it is in the Mother that it occurs. This is a very ancient belief, this return to the Mother figure, the Goddess of all Things. As Marija Gimbutas noted, there is no father figure in prehistory.

Perhaps the reign of the Father Gods is coming to an end, and the Goddess really is returning. For some neo-pagan feminists, she has never been away. She has simply been suppressed, like so many things. The Goddess in primæval times was a 'vast, dark, semiliquid mass of potential energy and matter intermixed', wrote Barbara G. Walker.[4] Redgrove tapped into this primæval energy when he is in the post-orgasmic trance, and expressed it in poems such as 'Orgasm', 'The Brilliance', 'Silver Women' and 'Her Shirt Open'.

For Redgrove, menstrual sex is the way in to the 'mother-world' when all the senses are acutely and gloriously opened. 'Somehow she opens certain doors in the air', he noted in 'The Golden Policeman' (SP, 173). This kind of lovemaking has many names in different cultures. Ginette Paris, for example, speaks of the gold and pink coloured sexuality of the Goddess Aphrodite, which is a form of magical sex.[5]

Peter Redgrove draws on many traditions of sex magic:

(1) on Taoism and Tantrism, and *maithuna,* which emphasize the Left Hand path, where the male-female forces of *shiva-shakti* and *yin-yang* are united by *kundalini* yoga and breath control;

(2) on sexual alchemy, where the 'Great Work' (of alchemy) is the sexual transformation of the male-female forces, here termed the king and queen or brother and sister;

(3) on Hebrew *horasis* and the *shekinah* of Qabbalism;

(4) on Gnostic Sophia magic;

(5) on Crowleyan sex magicke;
(6) on Dianism, as well as other forms of sex magic (BG,124-168).

There are many, many kinds of sex magic, amply explored by many writers.[6] In a letter to me of 1992, Redgrove explained what is desired in sex magic:

> What one wants to aim for is the 'staircase' with the man controlling his ejaculation and following with mini-climaxes the woman's sequential orgasms until they take each other... One may gently and courteously petition within [and] before sex (this is the sex magick) and watch what happens during or in the afterglow. This is not to be taken as a right or technique, but as sexual prayer.[7]

The goal is this bliss, sometimes called the 'Magickal Child', as opposed to the flesh-and-blood child created during ovulation. It's a natural, creative, waking dream, in which the lovers can dream the same dream, 'and the most beautiful pictures of places you have visited seem to rise through the skin' ("Greening the Orgasm", 30). It's a moment when '[e]verything | Inside us begins to rejoice', as Redgrove put it in 'More Than Meets the Eye' (Tar, 25).

For some, this menstrual, magical, transformative sex, where the 'exiled Black Goddess of supersensible eroticism (BG, 166) is brought back into the foreground of life, can be seen as sexist and heterosexual, without allowing for (or encouraging) other forms of eroticism (such as gay and lesbian sexuality). Further, it focuses on sex not love, which annoys some people.[8] Also, it does not operate within the spiritual and social contexts of a religion, which some people may find unsettling.

Actually, Peter Redgrove has created his own religion or cult. All artists do this. The shaman, as anthropologists state, is both the god/ creator and the priest/ servant of her/ his cult.[9] And Redgrove's cult of sex magicke is firmly situated within the traditions of mainstream religion, within age-old occultism and magic – as found in Tantrism, Taoism, Hinduism, Gnosticism, Qabbalism, and so on.

Some feminists will like Peter Redgrove's sex magic, because it

SEX–MAGIC–POETRY–CORNWALL

empowers the woman ('Women are divinities, they are life', said no less an authority than the Buddha.)[10] Other feminists will find Redgrove's sex alchemy limiting in its sexual role-playing and gender stereotyping. This kind of sex yoga is not alien to certain strands of Catholicism, for instance. Meinrad Craighead, working within the Christian mystical tradition, wrote: '[o]ur spirituality should centre on the affirmation of our female sexuality in its seasons of cyclic change.'[11] Many feminists embrace both Christianity and sexuality, both occultism and the body.

Peter Redgrove's alchemy of sex is closest to Taoism. Goddess worship is close to Taoism in its worldview (S. Nicholson, 19). The *Tao Te Ching* speaks of 'knowing the feminine'. The Black Goddess is quite at home in Taoism too, for the *Tao Te Ching* embraces the dark side of the feminine: 'keep to the feminine', the *Tao Te Ching* says, 'keep to the black'.[12] French feminists such as Julia Kristeva have found a different, deeper sexual connection between men and women in Far Eastern countries (see Kristeva's *About Chinese Women*, for instance).[13]

Redgrove's holistic view is Taoist, where all things are interlinked, and a spirit pervades everything: this is the Goddess. One can see that Taoist unification of the cosmos in *The Alchemical Journal* where, after lovemaking, all number of things are linked by the poetry of orgasm: the house, underground caves, clouds, ghosts, jewels, a herb garden after rain, etc. Orgasm is the ecstatic energy that links the world together poetically. These thoughts are not exclusive to Redgrove's poetry. Marge Piercy writes in a poem, 'Raining Pumpernickel': '[y]our love comes down rich as the warm spring rain'.[14] And Laura Chester wrote in a Redgrovean mode: '[y]our pheromone's my one cologne' (ib., 112), and Sue Miller wrote of sex thus: '[i]n those early mornings it all tasted of sex after a few moments... The whole room seemed full of our commingled, complicated smells' (ib.,101). This flowing, perfumed bliss is dependent on the woman – the 'mediatrix' as Redgrove calls her (TLS), the 'mistress of visions' as he put it in the poem 'On Having No Head' (Ark, 199).

Lawrence Durrell became interested in Taoist love magic and made it a theme in his *The Avignon Quintet* (1974-85). Durrell explored very similar Taoist and Tantric notions of lovemaking in the *Quintet*, that fusion of Occident and Orient beliefs which was so popular in the 1970s and 1980s. In his book on his meeting with the writer Jolan Chang, author of *The Tao of Love and Sex*, a guidebook to Taoist love (predating the New Age Mind/ Body/ Spirit books), Durrell wrote:

> The gratification of the lovers lay on a different plane; by dint of mastering the orgasm one raised love to a higher frequency. One prolonged life, the immortal life which one was in honour to try and realize upon earth... In the love-making of which the Taoist doctrines there could supervene an orgasm without loss of the vital Taoist essence. It was a question not only of conscious practice but of rapport, of attachment – the whole precious transaction was lifted to a new height of intensity which could endure for hours at a time, if necessary, because the two spirits remained enmeshed in each other.[15]

5.2   Beyond Sex?

No, Peter Redgrove will not go beyond sex. The Redgrove-poet lives wholly in the body, like D.H. Lawrence's characters. Any worldview/ system/ religion/ poetry/ magic must embrace the body for Redgrove. If it doesn't, it's too abstract, too distanced, too unreal. Redgrove's poetry never loses touch of the body. One won't find political commentary, sociological analysis, mathematics, traditional philosophy, linguist investigations, finance, the media and melodrama in his poetry. For some people, this lack of politics or social commentary might be a deficiency, but Redgrove's real world is a different one from the so-called 'real' world of politics or even social issues. Redgrove's real world is that of apples, bees, clouds, oceans, hands and wombs. If that isn't 'real' enough for some people, they must be on the wrong planet. You might find broadcasting mentioned in Redgrove's work – but not relating to TV or radio in the way you'd expect – see the idiosyncratic idea in the poem 'Far Star', for example, which says: '[s]he was broadcast into this world via the lady transmitter' (IHS, 36), or the poem 'Waterworks as Broadcasting House' (Wo, 34).

Peter Redgrove was certainly attracted to radio as a poetic notion – the idea of radio waves permeating the environment, for instance, radio as an invisible stream of images and voices and sounds – as well as a medium for creative work (Redgrove wrote many radio plays, which the BBC performed and broadcast). In *The Cyclopean Mistress*, Redgrove describes radio waves as invisible rays which tumble over and through the hills 'like a stiff breeze of watered silk that we cannot see', and wonders if radio might be emitting energy as touches or scents, operating on a supersensual level (CM, 19-20).

For Redgrove, all the agony and ecstasy of being alive flows from women, from the 'mother-world'. As he wrote in *In the Country of the Skin*: '[t]here is a shape between her legs which smells of mountains scraping stationary clouds' (38). Redgrove's magical view of women, love, the feminine and the Goddess is cosmic, and extends, as the quote from *In the Country of the Skin* suggests, to the very farthest reaches of the universe. The Goddess's power expands to clouds, mountains, orchards, underworlds and the stars: '[m]enstruating, the stars are out' he wrote in the poem 'Starlight' (FE, 24).

The feminine infuses simply everything, somewhat in the pantheist tradition, where God and nature are identical – *Deus sive Natura* in Baruch Spinoza's words.[1] In a similar way, the Tao pervades everything, as does Brahma or Self in Hinduism. Pantheism is found in mystics such as Meister Eckhart, Dionysius the Areopagite, Jacob Boehme, Nicholas of Cusa, and any number of poets.

Peter Redgrove's religion of love is very close to Tantrism modulated by Taoism. In Hindu Tantra, the Goddess Shakti is all-pervasive: '[w]hatever power anything possesses, that is the Goddess', say the Tantric texts.[2] Redgrove was moving in this mystical all-in-one direction in his earliest poetry. In 'The Ferns' he wrote: '[a]ll's water' (For, 17). He could be saying 'all's the Goddess', for the mystical identification of the Goddess and the ocean is ancient (feminists such as Monica Sjöo and Barbara Walker speak of the Goddess as a primæval mass of energy, as I have noted).

Peter Redgrove knew it was crucial to cultivate experiences in the 'mother-world', to keep in touch with the feminine, as the *Tao Te Ching* put it. Redgrove was someone who tried to feminize himself in the Jungian manner. 'The second birth is through a spiritual mother', commented a post-Jungian thinker, Joseph Campbell, echoing the doctrine of the alchemist Paracelsus about being reborn through the mother. Diving into the spiritual mother means acknowledging all manner of dark powers, where 'all surfaces become depths'. As Redgrove said in *The Alchemical Journal*: 'I knew she was better than beautiful: she was magic' (AJ, no. 27).

Whether she's in the stars menstruating, or in the ocean dreaming, or in the clouds releasing 'skin-orgasms', the Goddess is everywhere, like the spirit of the universe, the Tao, or Brahma, or Shakti, or *shekinah*, or Sophia, or Isis. In *Philosopher and Skin*, a later prose piece, Redgrove wrote:

> Not an independent subject confronting an objective, alien world, but rather the so-called subjectivity, the ego or inner sanctum, and nature, and other people, and the whole world, emerge from a common ground, embracing both humans and nature. (EA, 140)

6

A Critical Appraisal of Peter Redgrove's Poetry

It is deeply unfashionable in some circles to interpret texts in terms of spirituality or religion, or to discuss religion and mysticism with anything less than total scepticism and detachment. So to say that this 'common ground', or source of all life, is the Goddess, is ridiculous for those critics. (Although the idea of 'Gaia', the ecological deity which is the Earth's consciousness, is not a new idea, invented by scientists in the 20th century, and Jean-Paul Sartre's global village of the mid-century is also nothing new).[1] Literary critics in the U.K., for example, detest such ideas. Most of them revere the grumpy librarian, Philip Larkin, as a great poet, and can't deal with anything wilder. When Robert Graves and Philip Larkin died around the same time (December, 1985), there was much attention in the press and media about Larkin, but little about Graves. This says it all about the provincial, small-minded, shabby nature of British lit'ry criticism, and criticism in general. It is very conservative. Like the Judæo-Christian religions, literary criticism defends itself fiercely against attacks from outside with threaten its stability. It takes years for wild talent to be normalized and woven into the fold (such as Arthur Rimbaud). Robert Graves is still depicted as a charming but bizarre poet; he is regarded as one of those English eccentrics. Philip Larkin, meanwhile, is beatified. Why? It's obvious: because Larkin flatters the critics' own views of themselves, a particular gloomy, middle-class view of Middle England. This is also one reason why there are so few 'great' women poets in the canon of literary figures: because women poets often write of things beyond male critics' experience or beliefs.

So Peter Redgrove, with his magical feminist synæsthesia, ain't gonna fit in to the British cosy-armchair pipe-and-tea net-curtains TV-news-soap-opera stiff-upper-lip suburban world. What would the literary establishment make of this:

> I have the flames
> in my cunt
> and would burn everything
> to get you

This poem, by Lily Pond,[2] is a world away from the sarky, dull, morbid, dusty male British kind of poetry. Using Peter Redgrove's and Penny Shuttle's psychological approach, we can see that Pond's poem is a cry of rage of love in the manner of Sappho stemming from menstrual hysteria, a menstrual mania which tears apart patriarchy and strikes out for the female 'wild zone'. I quote this poem to show that Redgrove's is not the only form of wild poetry around at the moment.

This is what Robert Graves does with Philip Larkin – blasts him away poetically. But Brit lit crits will have none of it, and they cling onto Larkin and his fellow mediocre versifiers (such as Andrew Motion, Tom Paulin, Craig Raine, Fleur Adcock, Carol Ann Duffy, Simon Armitage and all the other dull poets the press and literary establishment in the U.K. enshrine.)

The menstrual, feminine energy in female poets such as Sappho, Adrienne Rich, Lily Pond, Sylvia Plath, Anna Akhmatova, Louise Labé, Gaspara Stampa, Marie Tsvetayeva, Yü Hsüan-chi, Rabi'a and Chu Shu-chen simply cannot be contained or controlled by men, male critics or patriarchal culture. Their poetry is too wild, too strange (yet also everyday). Women poets get sidelined because men don't know what to do with them. If you get the impression that most British literary critics are wimpy, grey, bland, white, Anglo-Saxon, suburban, middle-class males, you are not far wrong. But even if the critics are not like this themselves, then most their criticism is: wimpy, grey, bland, white, Anglo-Saxon, middle-class, suburban and patriarchal. It's all *so boring*!

So poets such as T.S. Eliot, one of the most unerotic of all poets, gets glorified. And Philip Larkin. And John Betjeman. And A.L. Alvarez. Ted Hughes, for example, is canonized by critics because his worldview accords with theirs. He wrote in an earthy, violent, muscular, masculine, neo-Jungian and religious fashion, with his Biblical ithyphallic gods crawling through the planet's undergrowth at worm-level, like Herne the Hunter, or the Celtic god Cernunnos, or the Greek deity Pan. The Goddess is there in Hughes' poetry ('Who is this? | She reveals herself and is veiled', he wrote in *Gaudete* [*Selected Poems*, 158]). And a late, lengthy exploration of William Shakespeare took in the Goddess: *Shakespeare and the Goddess of Complete Being*. Hughes' view of love veered between delicate spirituality and violent sensuality. In 'Lovesong', he evoked a vicious kind of sex:

> His sucked out her whole past and future or tried to
> He had no other appetite
> She bit him she gnawed him she sucked
> She wanted him complete inside her (ib., 128)

Here the woman is the voracious whore of pornography, the woman and vagina as the death-bringing gateway to Hell, the woman as castrating mother.

SEX–MAGIC–POETRY–CORNWALL

Ted Hughes and Peter Redgrove, like W.B. Yeats and Robert Graves, used heaps of shamanism, Western magic, Jungian myth and psychology in their poesie. But Redgrove was the most feminized, Goddess-soaked (male) poet of his generation – beside him other British writers contemporary with him look positively masculinist in the extreme: Hughes, J.G. Ballard, Martin Amis, Jon Silkin, George MacBeth, Christopher Middleton and Geoffrey Hill.

All the 'great' and 'important' names of British poetry – Edwin Muir, John Betjeman, Vernon Watkins, R.S. Thomas, Philip Larkin, Douglas Dunn – I've read them and they're oh-so clever, and witty, and topical, but, really, of little value. After you've read Rainer Maria Rilke or Paul Éluard or Arthur Rimbaud, you don't bother reading many British poets. Except the odd one or two. Redgrove is one of those few. I rate Peter Redgrove highly because his poetry is open to perceptions, insights and experiences which the poetry establishment wrongly consigns to the fringe.

Illustrations

Of some places, themes, influences and associations
in the poetry of Peter Redgrove.

Some inspirations for Peter Redgrove's poetry:
clouds, trees, water, eroticism, stones, alchemy,
fields, Cornwall and the sea.

This page and over: *Clouds*, Jeremy Robinson, 2005-06

Skywalkers with immense tension of presence
And extreme visibility and invisibility as well,
The cascades roll past, turn dragonish and then
They are all simple lace very high
On a blue robe which darkens with emergency generating stations
Black as floating mines of coal.

(From 'Falmouth Clouds')

Stream, New Forest, 2004, by Jeremy Mark Robinson

Images of the great Cornish stone circle of Boscawen-Ûn, near Penzance, with its phallic, leaning central stone, above, and white granite 'mother-stone', below
(Jeremy Robinson, 1996)

Two views of the Cornwall that features in Peter Redgrove's poetry: the Helford River at Helford Passage, above, and the Lizard at Kynance, below. (Jeremy Robinson, 1993, 1996).

Field, Isle of Grain, 2006, Joe Arthurs

Wheatfields, 2004, by Jeremy Mark Robinson

The greatest possible touch, to bathe.
The wind bathing in the wheat,
The great invisible woman plunges
into the heavy tassels, into the wheat-smell
That is like straw baskets full of new bread;
The wheat splashes round her, it must cry out,
All the stems chafing, like an immense piano plunged into
Which continues playing as she swims…

(From 'Harvest')

Cornish Granite Stone, 2005 (from St Just), by Jeremy Mark Robinson

The sheeted sea coming ashore
And hanging its pictures up in the hedges,
Its unsalted portraits,

The surface of the sea doubling
As it opens into sleep,
A source among white sources, cresting.

(Peter Redgrove, from 'Round Pylons')

Hokusai school pictures: c. 1830 (above),
woodblock, 19th century (below).

Eric Gill, Lovers, Kneeling, 1920

Goddess art contemporary with Peter Redgrove's poetry. This page: Ana Mendieta, mid-1970s. Over: Niki de Sant-Phalle, 1967.

Niki de Saint-Phalle, *Black Venus*, 1967

Mercury as a woman, from *Quinta Essentia*, Leonhardt Thurneisser zum Thurn, 1570. Overleaf: alchemical vessels.

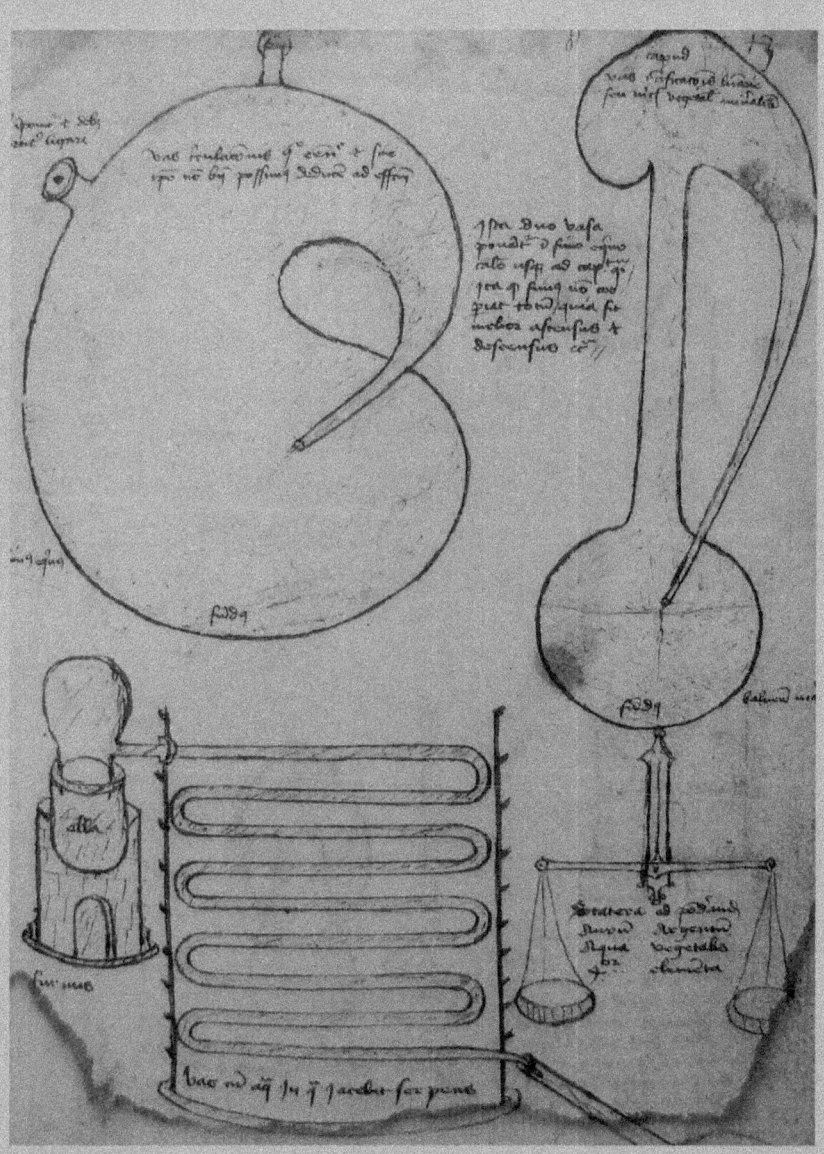

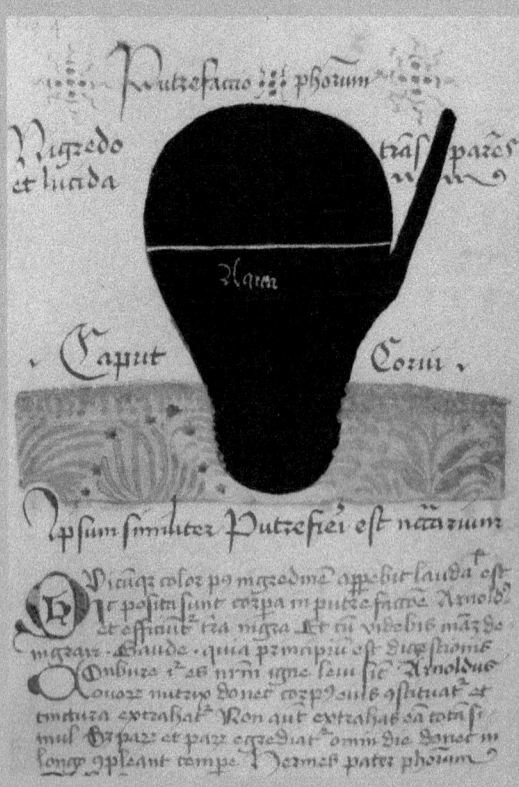

Alchemical texts. Above: Michael Maier, *Symbola aureæ mensæ*, Frankfurt, 1617, which features Hermes Tristmegistus.
Below: *Putrefacto philoosphurum*, Arnold of Villanova (British Library)

Alchemical texts. Below: Johann Daniel Mylius, *Anatomia auri*, Frankfurt, 1628. Above: *Conjunctio sive Coitus*, *Rosarium philosophorum*, Frankfurt, 1550.

Notes

One : The Inner and Outer Biography

1.1   Life / Influences / Context

1. See Martin Booth, 225f; E. Lucie-Smith, ed. *British Poetry Since 1945*, Penguin, London, 1985; various handbooks on contemporary writers, etc.
2. See P. Redgrove on Ted Hughes in interviews, "Lazarus and the Visionary Truth", "Scientist of the Strange", etc.
3. J.G. Ballard, *The Atrocity Exhibition*, Panther, London, 1967.
4. Letter to the author, March 14, 1993.
5. D.H. Lawrence, *Phoenix*, 355.

1.2   Psychology / Poetics

1. Letter to the author, ib.
2. See Laz, MR, PR, and other interviews.

1.3   Nature / Mysticism / Cornwall

1. Jacob Boehme, quoted in John Ferguson, 130.
2. Penelope Shuttle, talking of 'a threefold reality: of poetry: of love, erotic, spiritual...and of Cornwall (not England), weather and landscape and separateness' (*We Two*, 12).

SEX–MAGIC–POETRY–CORNWALL

Two : Alchemy of the Word

2.1   Rilke, Rimbaud, the Romantics and Redgrove

1. Novalis: *Pollen and Fragments: Selected Poetry and Prose*, tr. Arthur Versluis, Phanes Press, Grand Rapids, 1989, 64, 73.

2. R.M. Rilke: *Letters to Benvenuta*, tr. H. Norden, Hogarth Press, London, 1953, 51.

3. R.M. Rilke, "Primal Sound", in H.M. Block & H. Salinger, eds. *The Creative Vision: Modern European Writers*, Grove Press, New York, NY, 1960, 50.

4. R.M. Rilke: *Sonnets to Orpheus*, tr. J.B. Leishman, Hogarth Press, London, 1946, 59.

5. R.M. Rilke: 'The Bowl of Roses', in *New Poems*, tr. J.B.Leishman, Hogarth Press, London, 1963, 57.

6. See James Cowan: *The Mysteries of the Dream-Time*, Prism Press, 1989; Bruce Chatwin: *The Songlines*, Picador, London, 1988; Lucien Lévy-Bruhl: *Primitive Mythology*, University of Queensland Press, 1983.

2.2   Poetry and Life: The Strangeness of Strangeness

1. *Reflections on the Death of a Porcupine*, in *A Selection From Phoenix*, 456-7.

2. P. Redgrove, letter to the author, March 5, 1993.

3. Chuang-tzu: *Basic Writings*, tr. Watson, Columbia University Press, New York, NY.

4. R.M. Rilke: *Sonnets to Orpheus*, 106-7. And see H. Holthusen: *Rilke*, Bowes, 1952; Donald Prater: *A Ringing Glass: The Life of Rainer Maria Rilke*, Oxford University Press, Oxford, 1986.

5. P. Redgrove, quoted in Erika Duncan.

6. R.M. Rilke: *Briefe aus Muzot, 1921-26*, Insel Verlag, Leipzig, 1937, 333-4.

7. Letter to the author, April 14, 1993.

Hélene Cixous spoke about the poetic importance of dreaming, in relation to E.T.A. Hofmannsthal's book *The Wanderer*, in which the narrator meets a strange traveller:

> This man has apparently been walking for centuries, he is never named, but when you have lived in the country of poets, you immediately recognize who he is: he is Rimbaud. To meet Rimbaud we have to walk to Austria, to the Greece that is hidden within Austria; we have to travel to the heart of the

SEX–MAGIC–POETRY–CORNWALL

country of the unconscious, where we may again find those countries we have lost, including Algeria and the Jardin d'Essais. But for this we have to walk, to use our whole body to enable the world to become flesh, exactly as this happens in our dreams. In dreams and writing our body is alive: we either use the whole of it or, depending on the dream, a part. We must embark on body-to-body journeys in order to discover the body. (1993, 64-65)

Cixous adds, in a statement, that

In order to go to the School of Dreams, something must be displaced, starting with the bed. One has to get going. This is what writing is, starting off. It has to do with activity and passivity. This does not mean one will get there. Writing is not arriving; most of the time it's *not arriving*. One must go on foot, with the body. One has to go away, leave the self. How far must one not arrive in order to write, how far must one wander and wear out and have pleasure? One must walk as far as the night. One's own night. Walking through the self toward the dark. (ib.)

2.3   Shamanism

1. Robert Graves: *On English Poetry*, 19; *The White Goddess*, 12.
2. Weston La Barre: *The Ghost Dance*, Allen & Unwin, London, 1972.
3. A. Rimbaud, *Complete Works*, 305-311.

2.4   The Colours of Alchemy

1. See J.E. Cirlot, *A Dictionary of Symbols*, Routledge, London, 1981.

2.5   Deschooling of the Senses

1. A. Rimbaud, 1966, 307.
2. D.H. Lawrence: *Why the Novel Matters*, in *Phoenix*, 188.

2.7   The Language of Ecstasy

1. J.C. Powys: *Autobiography*, Macdonald, London, 1967, 168-9.
2. H.W. Fawkner, 150.
3. J.C. Powys: *In Defence of Sensuality*, Gollancz, London, 1930, 169.
4. P. Redgrove, letter to the author, March 5, 1993.

SEX–MAGIC–POETRY–CORNWALL

6. G. Wilson Knight: *The Saturnian Quest: John Cowper Powys*, Harvester Press, Sussex, 1978, and *Neglected Powers*, Routledge & Kegan Paul, London, 1972.

7. See Robert Graves's *The White Goddess*; and essays on the anvil, harp, hammer and oar of poetry in *Steps*; *The Crowning Privilege*; and *Poetic Craft and Principle*.

Three : Adventures in the Mother-World

1. *Selected Poems*, 50.

3.1   The Sixth Sense

1. See *Poems About Love*; *Mammon and the Black Goddess*.
On Robert Graves and his 'Muse-women', see Jeremy Mark Robinson: *Blinded By Her Light: The Love-Poetry of Robert Graves*, Crescent Moon, 1994; Patrick Keane: *A Wild Civility: Interactions in the Poetry and Thought of Robert Graves*, University of Missouri Press, Columbia, 1980; *Conversations With Robert Graves*, University of Mississippi Press, Jackson, 1989.

2. Max Beckmann, lecture, 1936, in H. B. Chipp, ed. *Theories of Modern Art*, University Of California Press, Los Angeles, CA, 1968, 188.

3. In Erika Duncan.

4. Mircea Eliade: *Ordeal By Labyrinth*, University of Chicago Press, Chicago, IL, 1984; *A History of Religious Ideas*, I, Collins, London, 1979.

3.2   Clouds

1. R. Graves: "The White Goddess", lecture, 1957, in *Steps*, 96.

2. "On *The Apple-Broadcast*", 166-7.

3. See Jeremy Mark Robinson: *Glorification: Religious Abstraction in Renaissance and 20th Century Painting*, Crescent Moon, 1990; Maurice Tuchman: *The Spiritual in Art: Abstract Painting 1880-1985*, Los Angeles County Museum of Art, LA, CA, 1986.

4. See Benjamin Walker: *Body Magic*, Granada, London, 1979.

5. 'Annalee and Her Sister', *The Laborators*, 46 (my italics).

SEX–MAGIC–POETRY–CORNWALL

3.3   Sex/ Weather/ Clothes/ Body

1. See Toril Moi: *Sexual/ Textual Politics: Feminist Literary Criticism*, Methuen, London, 1985, and Mary Eagleton, ed. *Feminist Literary Criticism*, Longman, London, 1991.

3.4   Magic

1. See Richard Cavendish: *The Magical Arts*, Arkana, London, 1984.
2. 'Nature is a temple where living pillars Let sometimes emerge confused words; Man crosses it through forests of symbols Which watch him with intimate eyes. Like those deep echoes that meet from afar In a dark and profound harmony, As vast as night and clarity, So perfumes, colors, tones answer each other. There are perfumes fresh as children's flesh, Soft as oboes, green as meadows, And others, corrupted, rich, triumphant, Possessing the diffusion of infinite things, Like amber, musk, incense and aromatic resin, Chanting the ecstasies of spirit and senses.' (tr. G. Wagner, *Selected Poems of Charles Baudelaire*, Grove Press, 1974).
3. Friedrich Hölderlin, like Arthur Rimbaud, Rilke and Redgrove, had an exalted view of the poet; they believed in the notion of the poet as shaman, a *sacer vates* or *poeta theologus*, a prophet, the high priest of people, more Blake than Wordsworth (L.S. Salzberger, 8-12). Hölderlin related the *sacer vates* to poets such as Ronsard, Sidney, Vida, Milton, Klopstock and Tasso (ib., 11).
4. H. Cixous, in E. Marks, 246-7.
5. H. Cixous, DJ, 23.
6. H. Cixous, "Preface", C, xv.
7. Hélène Cixous wrote about writing if describing the Rimbaudian or Redgrovean type of poet:

> I need writing [Rimbaud did too, for a while]; I need to surprise myself living [Rimbaud demanded this of poetry, but it couldn't deliver; Redgrove used poetry as a means of recording life's wonders]: I need to feel myself quiver with living [think of Rimbaud's 'deschooling of the senses, or Redgrove's poetic trances]: I need to call myself into living and to answer myself by living: I need to be living in the present of the present [Rimbaud knew this was the only place to live]: I need double-living: I need to come into life [this was Rimbaud's aim in his disaffected teenage]: I am afraid that writing will take the place of living [Rimbaud, realizing this problem, jettisoned writing; for Redgrove, they were part of the same thing]: I need writing thinking of

living; I wrote celebrating living [Redgrove's and Rimbaud's poetry is always celebration]

(*(With) Ou l'art de l'innocence* [*(With) Or the art of innocence*], 1981, in *The Hélène Cixous Reader*, 1994, 95)

This is pure Rimbaud, more of Rimbaud than Rimbaud himself. And of course Rimbaud *did* follow this ancient command of freeing oneself from every kind of shackle. His project was indeed to destroy all shackles, ties, ropes, laws, rules, boundaries, limits, dogmas, doctrines.

8. Patrick Süskind: *Perfume*, Penguin, London, 1987.

9. J.C. Powys: *Wolf Solent*, Penguin, London, 1964, 632.

3.5   Underworld / Underlife

1. See R.C. Zaehner: *Mysticism Sacred and Profane*, Oxford University Press, Oxford, 1957.

2. See A.J. Arberry: *Sufism*, Allen & Unwin, London, 1979.

3. R. Graves: *The White Goddess*, 341, 488; *Poetic Craft*, 109; *Steps*, 113.

4. See Hyder Rollins, ed. *A New Variorum Edition of Shakespeare: The Sonnets*, 2 vols, Lippincott, Philadelphia, PA, 1944; Joseph Pequingey: *Such Is My Love: A Study of Shakespeare's Sonnets*, University of Chicago Press, Chicago, IL, 1985.

5. D.H. Lawrence: *The Rainbow*, Penguin, London, 1986, 185.

Four : The Goddess and Feminisms

1. In S. Nicholson, 91.

4.1   The Return of the Goddess – Again

1. Merlin Stone, in S. Nicholson.

2. Chris Knight: *Blood Relations*, Yale University Press, New Haven, CT, 1991.

3. Judy Chicago, lecture, 1980, in Corrine Robbins: *The Pluralist Era: American Art 1968-1981*, Harper & Row, New York, NY, 1984, 53.

4. Some of the best books around on the Goddess include: Elinor Gadon: *The Once and Future Goddess*, Aquarian Press, Northants, 1990; Shirley Nicholson, ed. (see bibliography); Barbara G. Walker: *The Woman's Encyclopaedia of*

Myths and Secrets, Harper & Row, San Francisco, CA, 1983; Esther Harding: *Women's Mysteries*, Rider, London, 1989. Harding's book was cited admiringly in Redgrove and Shuttle's *Alchemy For Women.*

5. Ean Begg: *The Cult of the Black Virgin*, Routledge, London, 1985.

6. R. Graves in *Mammon and the Black Goddess*, 147; the Foreword to *Poems About Love*, 5.

7. R. Graves, *Collected Poems*, 331.

8. Plato: *Symposium*, tr. Jowett, in Maurice Valency: *In Praise of love: An Introduction to the Love-Poetry of the Renaissance*, Macmillan, New York, NY, 1961, 27.

9. *The Gospel According to Thomas*, quoted in S. Nicholson, 49.

10. Redgrove says the same thing of Jesus (in MR).

11. See John Groom: "Are we all descended from one woman?", *The Listener*, February 27, 1986, 10-11; Judith Cleeson: "Oya: Black Goddess of Africa", in S. Nicholson, 56, 67.

12. Bertrand Russell: *A History of Western Philosophy*, Allen & Unwin, London, 1971.

4.2   Feminism

1. In M. Eagleton, 81.

2. Luce Irigaray: *Ce sexe qui n'en est pas un*, Minuit, Paris 1977, in E. Marks 103.

3. In ib., 100.

4. Hélène Cixous: *Le jeune née*, UGE, Paris, 1975, in ib., 90f.

5. In S. Munt, 3-6.

6. Letter to the author, May 19, 1993.

7. In G. Chester, 169.

8. Andrea Dworkin: *Pornography: Men Possessing Women*, Women's Press, London, 1981, 23.

9. Alice Jardine: *Gynesis: Configurations of Women and Modernity*, Cornell University Press, Ithaca, NY, 1985.

10. Dale Spender: *Man-Made Language*, Routledge & Kegan Paul, London, 1985, 12f.

11. Hélène Cixous: "The Laugh of the Medusa", *Signs*, Summer 1976, in E. Marks, 253f.

12. See Mary Daly: *Pure Lust: Elemental Feminist Philosophy*, Women's Press, London, 1984, and her *Webster's First New Intergalactic Wickedary of the English Language*, Beacon Press, Boston, MA, 1987; Barbara G. Walker, op.cit.

13. H. Cixous, op.cit., 248.

14. Elaine Showalter: "Feminist Criticism in the Wilderness", in E. Showalter, ed. *The New Feminist Criticism*, Virago, London, 1986, 262-3.

15. In G. Chester, 139.

16. See Mary Daly: *Beyond God the Father*, Women's Press, London, 1985.

17. Julia Kristeva: *About Chinese Women*, in *The Kristeva Reader*, 1986, 154.

18. See Sarah Lucia Hoagland & Julia Penelope, eds. *For Lesbians Only: A separatist anthology*, Onlywomen Press, London, 1988; Marina Warner: *Monuments and Maidens*, Weidenfeld & Nicholson, London, 1985.

19. Joseph Campbell: *Power*, 167; Erich Neumann: *The Great Mother*, Princeton University Press, Princeton, NJ, 1972.

20. See M. Gimbutas; also Monica Sjöo & Barbara Mor: *The Great Cosmic Mother*, Harper & Row, San Francisco, CA, 1987.

21. M. Antonioni, in Sam Rohdie: *Antonioni*, British Film Institute, London, 1990, 183.

Five : Sex Magic, Sex Alchemy, Sex Yoga

5.1   Menstrual Sex

1. Letter to the author, September 16, 1993.

2. Quoted in C.G. Jung: *Psychology and Religion: East and West*, Routledge & Kegan Paul, London, 1977, 94.

3. Paracelsus, quoted in Mircea Eliade: *The Forge and the Crucible*, tr. Stephen Corrin, University of Chicago Press, Chicago, IL, 1978, 154.

4. Barbara G. Walker: *The I Ching of the Goddess*, Harper & Row, San Francisco, CA, 1986, 1.

5. Ginette Paris: *Pagan Meditations: The Worlds of Aphrodite, Artemis and Hestia*, Spring Publications, Dallas, Texas 1986, 26.

6. Redgrove recommends the following books on sex magic (among others): Stephen T. Chang: *The Tao of Sexuality*, Tao Publishing, 1986; Mantak Chia: *Taoist Secrets of Love*, Aurora Press, New York, NY, 1984; Louis T. Culling: *A Manual of Sex Magick*, Llewellyn Publications, Saint Paul, Minnesota, 1971; Margo Anand: *The Art of Sexual Ecstasy*, Aquarian Press, Northants, 1990.

7. Letter to the author, September 2, 1992.

8. A letter from Diana Johnston in *Resurgence* (no. 151, 45) criticizes Redgrove's article "Greening the Orgasm" (*Resurgence*, 150, Jan/ Feb 1992) thus: 'crude, insensitive and offensive to women... Redgrove's article is an end-gaining

exercise, i.e. climax orientated and concerned only with the multi-orgasmic couple "taking each other"'.

9. Weston La Barre: 'the shaman-artist creates his cult and his god', *The Ghost Dance*, op.cit., 352.

10. De La Vallé Poussin: *Bouddhisme: études et matériaux*, Paris, 1898, 144; and see Julius Evola: *The Metaphysics of Sex*, East-West Publications, 1983, 241.

11. In Mary Giles, ed. *The Feminist Mystic*, Crossroad, New York, NY, 1986, 79.

12. *Tao Te Ching*, tr. D.C. Lau, Penguin, London, 1963, 83.

13. Julia Kristeva: *About Chinese Women*, 1977.

14. In L. Chester, 124,

15. Lawrence Durrell: *A Smile In the Mind's Eye*, Wildwood House, 1980, 13, 18.

5.2   Beyond Sex?

1. Quoted in J. Ferguson, 138.
2. In J. Ferguson, 186.

Six: A Critical Appraisal of Peter Redgrove's Poetry

1. J. Campbell, *Power*, 179; J.-P. Sartre, in H.M. Block, op.cit.
2. Lily Pond: 'Ovulation', in L. Chester, 151.

Bibliography

Abbreviations appear after each entry

Peter Redgrove: Poetry

The Collector and Other Poems, Routledge & Kegan Paul, London, 1960
The Nature of Cold Weather and Other Poems, Routledge and Kegan Paul, London, 1961 [NCW]
At the White Monument and Other Poems, Routledge & Kegan Paul, London, 1963 [WM]
The God-Trap, Turret Books, London, 1966
The Force and Other Poems, Routledge & Kegan Paul, London, 1966 [For]
The Sermon, Poet & Printer, London, 1966
Work in Progress, Poet & Printer, London, 1969
Penguin Modern Poets 11 (with D.M. Black & D.M. Thomas), Penguin, 1968
The Mother, the Daughter and the Sighing Bridge, Sycamore Press, 1970
The Bedside Clock, Sycamore Press, London, 1971
Three Pieces For Voices, Poet and Printer, 1972
Dr Faust's Sea-Spiral Spirit and Other Poems, Routledge & Kegan Paul, London, 1972 [Dr]
*In the Country of the Skin: A Radio Scrip*t, Peter Redgrove, Falmouth, 1973 [ICS]
Words, Words Press, 1974
Sons of My Skin: Redgrove's Selected Poems 1954-1974, ed. M. Peel, Routledge & Kegan Paul, London, 1975
From Every Chink of the Ark and other new poems, Routledge & Kegan Paul, London, 1977 [Ark]
Skull Event, Sceptre Press, Knotting, 1977
Ten poems, Words Press, 1977

SEX–MAGIC–POETRY–CORNWALL

The Fortifiers, the Vitrifiers and the Witches, Sceptre Press, 1977
Happiness, Priapus, 1978
The White, Night-Flying Moths Called Souls, Sceptre Press, Knotting, 1978
The Weddings at Nether Powers and other new poems, Routledge & Kegan Paul, London, 1979 [WNP]
The Apple-Broadcast and other new poems, Routledge & Kegan Paul, London, 1981 [AB]
Cornwall in Verse, ed. P. Redgrove, Secker & Warburg, London, 1982
The Working of Water, Taxus Press, Durham, 1984 [WW]
The Man Named East and other new poems, Routledge & Kegan Paul, London, 1985 [Man]
The Mudlark Poems and Grand Buveur, Rivelin Grapheme Press, 1986 [Mud]
Explanation of Two Visions: Poems, Sixth Chamber Press, 1986
In the Hall of the Saurians, Secker & Warburg, London, 1987 [IHS]
Poems 1954-1987, Penguin, London, 1989 [Sel]
The First Earthquake, Secker & Warburg, London, 1989 [FE]
Dressed As For a Tarot Pack, Taxus, Exeter, 1990 [Tar]
Under the Reservoir, Secker & Warburg, London, 1992 [UR]
The Laborators, Stride, Exeter, 1993 [Lab]
My Father's Trapdoors, Cape, London, 1994
Abyssophone, Stride, Exeter, 1995
Sex-Magic-Poetry-Cornwall: A Flood of Poems, ed. and essay by J. Robinson, Crescent Moon, 1994
Assembling a Ghost, Cape, London, 1996
The Best of Peter Redgrove's Poetry: The Book of Wonders, ed. J. Robinson, Crescent Moon, 1996
What the Black Mirror Saw, Stride, Exeter, 1997
Orchard End, Stride, Exeter, 1997
Selected Poems, Cape, London, 1999
From the Virgil Caverns, Cape, London, 2002
Sheen, Stride, Exeter, 2003
A Speaker For the Silver Goddess, Stride, Exeter, 2006
The Harper, Jonathan Cape, London, 2006

SEX–MAGIC–POETRY–CORNWALL

Peter Redgrove: Prose

In the Country of the Skin, Routledge & Kegan Paul, London, 1973/ Stride, Exeter, 2006
Miss Carstairs Dressed For Blooding and Other Plays, Boyars, London, 1976
The God of Glass: A Morality, Routledge & Kegan Paul, London, 1979/ Stride, Exeter, 2006
The Sleep of the Great Hypnotist: The Life and Death and Life After Death of a Modern Magician, Routledge & Kegan Paul, London, 1979/ Stride, Exeter, 2006
The Beekeepers, Routledge & Kegan Paul, London, 1980/ Stride, Exeter, 2006
Martyr of the Hives, in *Best Radio Plays of 1980*, BBC Publications, London, 1981
The Facilitators or, Madam Hole-in-the-Day, Routledge & Kegan Paul, London, 1982/ Stride, Exeter, 2006
Time For the Cat-Scene in Words, *The New Literary Forum*, 5, Oct 1985, 6, Nov, 1985
The One Who Set Out to Study Fear, Bloomsbury, London, 1989
"The Cyclopean Mistress – Short Fiction, or Prose Poem? - An Argument in Progress", 1990, unpublished
An Alchemical Journal, 1990, unpublished MS, and in *The Cyclopean Mistress* [A]
A Crystal of Industrial Time, *Manhattan Review*, 1990, 59-62 [CIT]
Eight Alcameos, *Sulfur* (29), Winter, 1991-92, 133-140 [EA]
"The Cyclopean Mistress", "Greedy Green", "Strong Sugar", "The Model", "Cold University" [prose pieces], *Proposition* (4), 1991 [Pro]
"Introducing Peter Redgrove", *Poetry USA*, 24, 1992
The Cyclopean Mistress: Selected Short Fiction 1960-1990, Bloodaxe Books, Newcastle, 1993 [CM]

Peter Redgrove: Non-fiction

"Interview with Peter Redgrove", *Hudson Review*, 28, 3, Autumn, 1975 [Hud]
"A Poet in Teaching: A Personal Account", *New Universities Quarterly*, Spring, 1980
"The Dialogue of Gender: Penelope Shuttle and Peter Redgrove", in M. Wandor,

ed. *On Gender and Writing*, Pandora, London, 1983

"Scientist of the Strange: An Interview with Peter Redgrove", P. Fried, *Manhattan Review*, 3, 1, Summer, 1983 [SS]

"Lazarus and the Visionary Truth: An Interview with Peter Redgrove", C. Ashcroft, *Arrows* (Sheffield), 1984 [Laz]

"May Day at Padstow", "Effigy Burning", "Men, Menstruation and the Moon", in C. Rawlence, ed. *About Time*, Cape, London, 1985

"Peter Redgrove: The Science of the Subjective" [interview], *Poetry Review*, June, 1987, 4-10 [PR]

The Black Goddess and the Sixth Sense, Bloomsbury, London, 1987 [BG]

"On *The Apple Broadcast*", in J. Barker, ed. *Thirty Years of the Poetry Book Society 1956-1986*, Hutchinson, London, 1988, 166-7

"Work and Incubation: A Sketch of My Method of Writing", July, 1988, unpublished MS [WI]

[On poetry, women and feminism], article in *Times Literary Supplement*, 3-9 June, 1988 [TLS]

"Rimbaud My Virgil", *Sulfur* (30), Spring, 1992, 172-178

"Greening the Orgasm", *Resurgence* (150), Jan/ Feb, 1992, 30-33 [GO]

"Sisters on the sexual picket line [review of Chris Knight's *Blood Relations*]", *Times Literary Supplement*, 7 February, 1992, 21

"Interview with Peter Redgrove", *Pagan Voice*, 6, May, 1992, 4-5

"From *The Guest Father*", *Sulfur*, 34, Spring, 1994, 19-29

'Reader', in *Memes*, 9, April 1994, 41

The Colour of Radio: Essays and Interviews, ed. N. Roberts, Stride, Exeter, 2006

Peter Redgrove with Penelope Shuttle

The Hermaphrodite Album, Fuller d'Arch Smith, 1973

The Terrors of Dr Treviles: A Romance, Routledge & Kegan Paul, London, 1976/ Stride, Exeter, 2006

The Glass Cottage, Routledge & Kegan Paul, London, 1976/ Stride, Exeter, 2006

The Wise Wound: Menstruation and Everywoman, Paladin, London, 1986

The Menstrual Mandala, 1991, unpublished MS

"Peter Redgrove and Penelope Shuttle" [interview] *We Two: Couples talk about living, loving and working partnerships for the 90s*, ed. R. Housden & C. Goodchild, Aquarian Press/ Thorsons, 1992

SEX–MAGIC–POETRY–CORNWALL

"How We Met", interview by E. Oxford, *The Independent on Sunday*, 16 August, 1992, 61

Alchemy For Women, Rider, London, 1995 [AFW]

Others

C. Ashcroft: "The Novels of Peter Redgrove", *Arrows*, Sheffield?, n.d.

P. Bentley. *Scientist of the Strange: The Poetry of Peter Redgrove*, Farleigh Dickinson University Press, 2002

M. Booth: *British Poetry 1964-1984: Driving Through the Barricades*, Routledge & Kegan Paul, London, 1985

J. Campbell: *The Power of Myth*, with b. Moyers, ed. b. Flowers, Doubleday, New York, NY, 1988

G. Chester & J. Dickey, eds. *Feminism and Censorship: The Current Debate*, Prism Press, Bridport, Dorset 1988

L. Chester, ed. *Deep Down: New Sensual Writing by Women*, Faber, London, 1988

H. Cixous. *The Newly Born Woman*, tr. Betsy Wing, Minnesota University Press, Minneapolis, 1986

—. *"Coming to Writing" and Other Essays*, tr. Sarah Cornell *et al*, Harvard University Press, Cambridge, 1991

—. *Three Steps on the Ladder of Writing*, tr. Sarah Cornell & Susan Sellers, Columbia University Press, New York, 1993

—. *The Hélène Cixous Reader*, ed. Susan Sellers, Routledge, 1994

E. Duncan: "Peter Redgrove and Penelope Shuttle: The Joys and Perils of Collaboration", *Book Forum*, vol. VII, no.4, 1986

M. Eagleton, ed. *Feminist Literary Criticism*, Longman, London, 1991

T. Eagleton. "Rituals of the Mind", *Times Literary Supplement*, Aug, 1987

M. Eliade: *Shamanism: Archaic Techniques of Ecstasy*, Princeton University Press, Princeton, NJ, 1972

H.W. Fawkner: *The Ecstatic World of John Cowper Powys*, Associated University Presses, Cranbury, NJ, 1986

J. Ferguson: *An Illustrated Encyclopaedia of Mysticism*, Thames & Hudson, London, 1976

J. Foley: "Introducing Peter Redgrove", *Poetry USA*, (24), 1992, Oakland, CA

M. Gimbutas: *The Language of the Goddess*, Thames & Hudson, London, 1989

R. Graves. *On English Poetry*, Heinemann, London, 1922

—. *Steps*, Cassell, London, 1958
—. *The Crowning Privilege*, Penguin, London, 1959
—. *The White Goddess*, Faber, London, 1961
—. *Mammon and the Black Goddess*, Cassell, London, 1965
—. *Poetic Craft and Principle*, Cassell, London, 1967
—. *Poems About Love*, Cassell, London, 1969
—. *Collected Poems*, Cassell, London, 1975
T. Hughes. *Poetry in the Making*, Faber, London, 1969
—. *Shakespeare and the Goddess of Complete Being*, Faber, London, 1992
Julia Kristeva. *About Chinese Women*, tr. A. Barrows, Boyars, 1977
—. *Desire in Language: A Semiotic Approach to Literature and Art*, ed. L.S. Roudiez, tr. Thomas Gora *et al*, Blackwell 1982
—. *Revolution in Poetic Language*, tr. Margaret Walker, Columbia University Press, New York, 1984
—. *The Kristeva Reader*, ed. Toril Moi, Blackwell 1986
—. *Tales of Love*, tr. L.S. Roudiez, Columbia University Press, New York, 1987
—. "A Question of Subjectivity: an interview" [with Susan Sellers], *Women's Review*, 12, 1986, in Rice, 1992
D.H. Lawrence: *A Selection From Phoenix*, ed. A.A.H. Inglis, Penguin, London, 1977
E. Marks & I. de Courtivron, eds. *New French Feminisms: An Anthology*, Harvester Wheatsheaf, London, 1981
A. Motion *et al*. *Full of Star's Dreaming: Peter Redgrove 1932-2003*, Stride, Exeter, 2003
S. Munt, ed. *New Lesbian Criticism: Literary and Cultural Readings*, Harvester Wheatsheaf, London, 1992
S. Nicholson, ed. *The Goddess Re-Awakening: The Feminine Principle Today*, Theosophical Publishing House, Wheaton, IL, 1989
G. Pawling. "Alchemy of the Green Man", *Delta*, 58, 1978
Michael Payne. *Reading Theory: An Introduction to Lacan, Derrida, and Kristeva*, Blackwell, 1993
Poetry Review (Peter Redgrove issue), ed. R. Garfitt, 71-72, 1981
A. Rimbaud: *Complete Works, Selected Letters*, tr. W. Fowlie, University of Chicago Press, Chicago, IL, 1966
N. Roberts. "Peter Redgrove", in S. Vice *et al*, eds. *Beyond the Pleasure Dome*, Sheffield Academic Press, Sheffield, 1994
—. *The Lover, the Dreamer and the World: The Poetry of Peter Redgrove*, Sheffield Academic Press, Sheffield, 1994
J.M. Robinson. *Here Comes the Flood: The Poetry of Peter Redgrove*, Crescent

SEX–MAGIC–POETRY–CORNWALL

Moon, 1996

L.S. Salzberger. *Hölderlin*, Cambridge University Press, Cambridge, 1952

P. Shuttle. *All the Usual Hours of Sleeping: A Novel*, Calder and Boyars, London, 1969

—. *Wailing Monkey Embracing a Tree*, Calder and Boyars, London, 1973

—. *Rainsplitter in the Zodiac Garden*, Marion Boyars, London, 1977

—. *The Orchard Upstairs*, Oxford University Press, Oxford, 1980

—. *The Mirror of the Giant*, Marion Boyars, London, 1980

—. *The Child-Stealer*, Oxford University Press, Oxford, 1983

—. *The Lion From Rio*, Oxford University Press, Oxford, 1986

—. *Adventures With My Horse*, Oxford University Press, Oxford, 1988

—. *Taxing the Rain*, Oxford University Press, Oxford, 1992

—. *Delicious Babies*, Circle Press, 1996

—. *Building a City for Jamie*, Oxford University Press, Oxford, 1996

—. *Redgrove's Wife*, Bloodaxe, Newcastle, 2006

M. Vassi. *The Erotic Comedies*, Black Spring Press, London, 1988

THE ART OF ANDY GOLDSWORTHY

COMPLETE WORKS: SPECIAL EDITION
(PAPERBACK and HARDBACK)

by William Malpas

A new, special edition of the study of the contemporary British sculptor, Andy Goldsworthy, including a new introduction, new bibliography and many new illustrations.

This is the most comprehensive, up-to-date, well-researched and in-depth account of Goldsworthy's art available anywhere.

Andy Goldsworthy makes land art. His sculpture is a sensitive, intuitive response to nature, light, time, growth, the seasons and the earth. Goldsworthy's environmental art is becoming ever more popular: 1993's art book *Stone* was a bestseller; the press raved about Goldsworthy taking over a number of London West End art galleries in 1994; during 1995 Goldsworthy designed a set of Royal Mail stamps and had a show at the British Museum. Malpas surveys all of Goldsworthy's art, and analyzes his relation with other land artists such as Robert Smithson, Walter de Maria, Richard Long and David Nash, and his place in the contemporary British art scene.

The Art of Andy Goldsworthy discusses all of Goldsworthy's important and recent exhibitions and books, including the *Sheepfolds* project; the TV documentaries; *Wood* (1996); the New York Holocaust memorial (2003); and Goldsworthy's collaboration on a dance performance.

Illustrations: 70 b/w, 1 colour. 330 pages. New, special, 2nd edition.
Publisher: Crescent Moon Publishing. Distributor: Gardners Books.

ISBN 1-86171-059-3 (9781861710598) (Paperback) £25.00 / $44.00

ISBN 1-86171-080-1 (9781861710802) (Hardback) £60.00 / $105.00

ANDY GOLDSWORTHY IN CLOSE-UP

SPECIAL EDITION (HARDBACK and PAPERBACK)

by William Malpas

A new, special edition of our bestselling title, exploring Andy Goldsworthy's artworks in detail. A good, all-round introduction to Goldsworthy's art.

Illustrations: 160 b/w, 4 colour. 260 pages. Second edition. Hardback. Publisher: Crescent Moon Publishing. Distributor: Gardners Books.

ISBN 1-86171-094-1 (9781861710949) (Hbk) £60.00 / $105.00

ISBN 1-86171-091-7 (9781861710919) (Pbk) £25.00 / $44.00

Available from bookstores. amazon.com, play.com, tesco.com, and other websites.
In the United States from Baker & Taylor, (800) 7753760 or (800) 7751100 or (908) 5417062. electser@btol.com or btinfo@btol.com.

ANDY GOLDSWORTHY

TOUCHING NATURE:
SPECIAL EDITION

(PAPERBACK and HARDBACK)

by William Malpas

A new, special and updated edition of our bestselling title, providing an excellent general introduction to the art of Andy Goldsworthy.

Illustrations: 75 b/w, 2 colour. 354 pages. Third edition. Paperback.

Publisher: Crescent Moon Publishing. Distributor: Gardners Books.

ISBN 1-86171-056-9 (9781861717) (Paperback) £25.00 / $44.00

ISBN 1-86171-087-9 (9781861710871) (Hardback) £60.00 / $105.00

THE ART OF RICHARD LONG

COMPLETE WORKS : SPECIAL EDITION
(HARDBACK and PAPERBACK)

by William Malpas

A new study of the British artist Richard Long, an important contemporary international artist. The most detailed, in-depth exploration of Richard Long's art currently available.

Illustrations: 48 b/w, 2 colour. 439 pages.
First edition. Hardback and paperback editions.

Publisher: Crescent Moon Publishing. Distributor: Gardners Books.

ISBN 1-86171-079-8 (9781861710796) (Hardback) £60.00 / $105.00

ISBN 1-86171-081-X (9781861710819) (Paperback) £25.00 / $44.00

LAND ART

A COMPLETE GUIDE TO LANDSCAPE, ENVIRONMENTAL, EARTHWORKS, NATURE, SCULPTURE AND INSTALLATION ART

by William Malpas

A new, special edition of our popular book on land art.
Chapters on land artists such as Robert Smithson, Walter de Maria, Christo, Michael Heizer, Richard Long and Andy Goldsworthy.

Illustrations: 35 b/w, 2 colour. 314 pages. First edition. Paperback.

Publisher: Crescent Moon Publishing. Distributor: Gardners Books.

ISBN 1-86171-062-3 (9781861710628) £25.00 / $44.00

J.R.R. Tolkien
The Books, The Films, The Whole Cultural Phenomenon

by Jeremy Mark Robinson

A new critical study of J.R.R. Tolkien, creator of Middle-earth and author of *The Lord of the Rings*, *The Hobbit* and *The Silmarillion*, among other books.

This new critical study explores Tolkien's major writings (*The Lord of the Rings*, *The Hobbit*, *Beowulf: The Monster and the Critics*, *The Letters*, *The Silmarillion* and *The History of Middle-earth* volumes); Tolkien and fairy tales; the mythological, political and religious aspects of Tolkien's Middle-earth; the critics' response to Tolkien's fiction over the decades; the Tolkien industry (merchandizing, toys, role-playing games, posters, Tolkien societies, conferences and the like); Tolkien in visual and fantasy art; the cultural aspects of The Lord of the Rings (from the 1950s to the present); Tolkien's fiction's relationship with other fantasy fiction, such as C.S. Lewis and *Harry Potter*; and the TV, radio and film versions of Tolkien's books, including the 2001-03 Hollywood interpretations of *The Lord of the Rings*.

This new book draws on contemporary cultural theory and analysis and offers a sympathetic and illuminating (and sceptical) account of the Tolkien phenomenon. This book is designed to appeal to the general reader (and viewer) of Tolkien: it is written in a clear, jargon-free and easily-accessible style.

754pp   ISBN 1-86171-057-7   £25.00 / $37.50

Walerian Borowczyk

Cinema of Erotic Dreams

by Jeremy Mark Robinson

Walerian Borowczyk (1923-2006) was a Polish artist, animator and filmmaker who lived in France for much of his life. He is the author of European art cinema masterpieces Goto: Island of Love, Blanche and Immoral Tales, some surreal animated shorts, and controversial films such as The Beast. This new book concentrates on Borowczyk's feature films, from Goto to Love Rites, which contain some of the most extraordinary images and scenes in recent cinema. Erotica for some, porn for others, Borowczyk's films are highly idiosyncratic and unforgettable.

Bibliography, notes, illustrations   240pp.
Paperback   ISBN 9781861712301   £15.00 / $30.00

Jean-Luc Godard

The Passion of Cinema / Le Passion de Cinéma

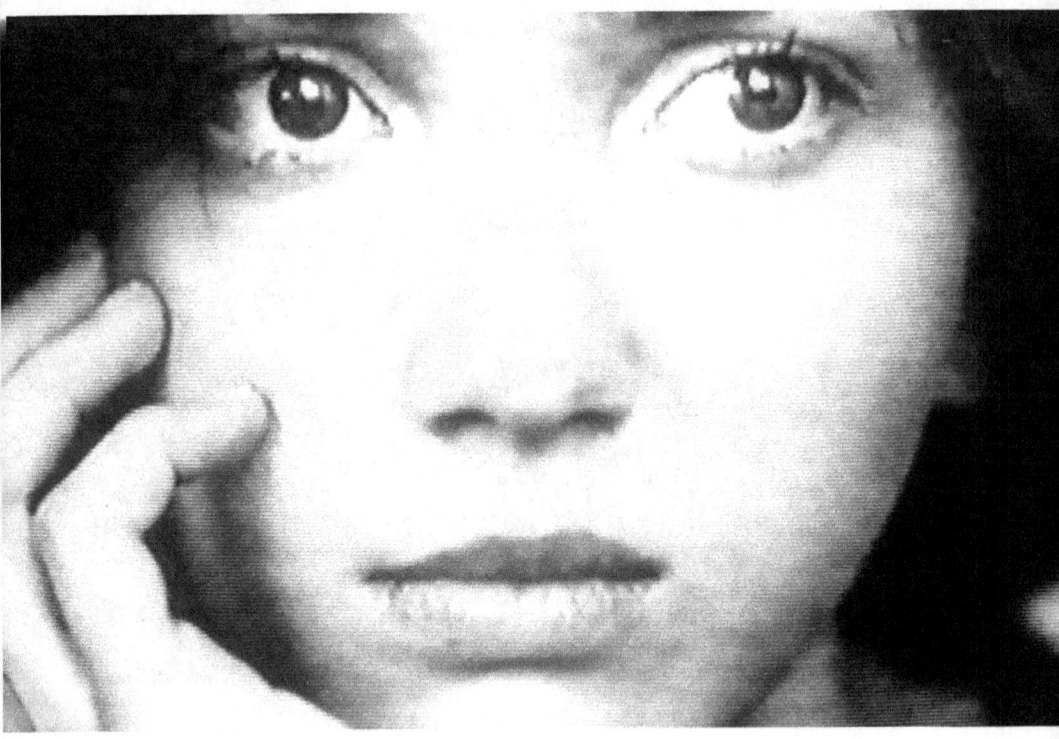

by Jeremy Mark Robinson

A new study of the French filmmaker Jean-Luc Godard (b. 1930), director of iconic films such as *Breathless, Weekend, Pierrot le Fou, Passion* and *Vivre Sa vie*. This book explores 27 of Godard's major films, from *Breathless* to *Notre Musique*, and includes a scene by scene analysis of Godard's controversial 1985 movie of the Virgin Mary, *Je Vous Salue, Marie*.

Bibliography, notes, illustrations   420pp
Hardback   ISBN 9781761712271   £50.00 / $100.00

THE SACRED CINEMA OF ANDREI TARKOVSKY

by Jeremy Mark Robinson

A new study of the Russian filmmaker Andrei Tarkovsky (1932-1986), director of seven feature films, including *Andrei Roublyov, Mirror, Solaris, Stalker* and *The Sacrifice*.
This is one of the most comprehensive and detailed studies of Tarkovsky's cinema available. Every film is explored in depth, with scene-by-scene analyses. All aspects of Tarkovsky's output are critiqued, including editing, camera, staging, script, budget, collaborations, production, sound, music, performance and spirituality. Tarkovsky is placed with a European New Wave tradition of filmmaking, alongside directors like Ingmar Bergman, Carl Theodor Dreyer, Pier Paolo Pasolini and Robert Bresson.
An essential addition to film studies.

Illustrations: 150 b/w, 4 colour. 682 pages. First edition. Hardback.

Publisher: Crescent Moon Publishing. Distributor: Gardners Books.

ISBN 1-86171-096-8 (9781861710963) £60.00 / $105.00

Life, Life
Selected Poems

Arseny Tarkovsky

translated and edited by Virginia Rounding

Arseny Tarkovsky is the neglected Russian poet, father of the acclaimed film director Andrei Tarkovsky. This new book gathers together many of Tarkovsky's most lyrical and heartfelt poems, in Rounding's clear, new translations. Many of Tarkovsky's poems appeared in his son's films, such as *Mirror, Stalker, Nostalghia* and *The Sacrifice*. There is an introduction by Rounding, and a bibliography of both Arseny and Andrei Tarkovsky.

Bibliography and notes   110pp   2nd ed   ISBN 1-86171-114-X   £10.00 / $20.00

In the Dim Void

Samuel Beckett's Late Trilogy: *Company, Ill Seen, Ill Said* and *Worstward Ho*

by Gregory Johns

This book discusses the luminous beauty and dense, rigorous poetry of Beckett's late works, *Company, Ill Seen, Ill Said* and *Worstward Ho*. Johns looks back over Beckett's long writing career, charting the development from the *Molloy-Malone Dies-Unnamable* trilogy through the 'fizzles' of the 1960s to the elegiac lyricism of the *Company* series. Johns compares the trilogy with late plays such as *Ghosts*, *Footfalls* and *Rockaby*.

Bibliography, notes. 120pp
ISBN 1861710712 and ISBN 1861712356   £10.00 / $20.00

CRESCENT MOON PUBLISHING

ARTS, PAINTING, SCULPTURE

The Art of Andy Goldsworthy: Complete Works
Andy Goldsworthy: Touching Nature
Andy Goldsworthy in Close-Up
Andy Goldsworthy: Pocket Guide
Andy Goldsworthy In America
Land Art: A Complete Guide
Richard Long: The Art of Walking
The Art of Richard Long: Complete Works
Richard Long in Close-Up
Richard Long: Pocket Guide
Land Art In the UK
Land Art in Close-Up
Land Art In the U.S.A.
Land Art: Pocket Guide
Installation Art in Close-Up
Minimal Art and Artists In the 1960s and After
Colourfield Painting
Land Art DVD, TV documentary
Andy Goldsworthy DVD, TV documentary
The Erotic Object: Sexuality in Sculpture From Prehistory to the Present Day
Sex in Art: Pornography and Pleasure in Painting and Sculpture
Postwar Art
Sacred Gardens: The Garden in Myth, Religion and Art
Glorification: Religious Abstraction in Renaissance and 20th Century Art
Early Netherlandish Painting
Leonardo da Vinci
Piero della Francesca
Giovanni Bellini
Fra Angelico: Art and Religion in the Renaissance
Mark Rothko: The Art of Transcendence
Frank Stella: American Abstract Artist
Jasper Johns: Painting By Numbers
Brice Marden
Alison Wilding: The Embrace of Sculpture
Vincent van Gogh: Visionary Landscapes
Eric Gill: Nuptials of God
Constantin Brancusi: Sculpting the Essence of Things
Max Beckmann
Caravaggio
Gustave Moreau
Egon Schiele: Sex and Death In Purple Stockings
Delizioso Fotografico Fervore: Works In Process 1
Sacro Cuore: Works In Process 2
The Light Eternal: J.M.W. Turner
The Madonna Glorified: Karen Arthurs

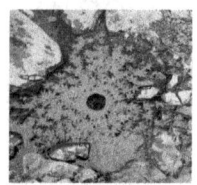

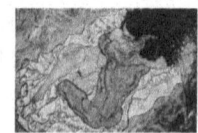

LITERATURE

J.R.R. Tolkien: The Books, The Films, The Whole Cultural Phenomenon
J.R.R. Tolkien: Pocket Guide
Tolkien's Heroic Quest
The *Earthsea* Books of Ursula Le Guin
Beauties, Beasts and Enchantment: Classic French Fairy Tales
Sexing Hardy: Thomas Hardy and Feminism
Thomas Hardy's *Tess of the d'Urbervilles*
Thomas Hardy's *Jude the Obscure*
Thomas Hardy: The Tragic Novels
Love and Tragedy: Thomas Hardy
The Poetry of Landscape in Hardy
Wessex Revisited: Thomas Hardy and John Cowper Powys
Wolfgang Iser: Essays and Interviews
Petrarch, Dante and the Troubadours
Maurice Sendak and the Art of Children's Book Illustration
Andrea Dworkin
Cixous, Irigaray, Kristeva: The *Jouissance* of French Feminism
Julia Kristeva: Art, Love, Melancholy, Philosophy, Semiotics and Psychoanalysis
Hélene Cixous I Love You: The *Jouissance* of Writing
Luce Irigaray: Lips, Kissing, and the Politics of Sexual Difference
Peter Redgrove: Here Comes the Flood
Peter Redgrove: Sex-Magic-Poetry-Cornwall
Lawrence Durrell: Between Love and Death, East and West
Love, Culture & Poetry: Lawrence Durrell
Cavafy: Anatomy of a Soul
German Romantic Poetry: Goethe, Novalis, Heine, Hölderlin
Feminism and Shakespeare
Shakespeare: Love, Poetry & Magic
The Passion of D.H. Lawrence
D.H. Lawrence: Symbolic Landscapes
D.H. Lawrence: Infinite Sensual Violence
Rimbaud: Arthur Rimbaud and the Magic of Poetry
The Ecstasies of John Cowper Powys
Sensualism and Mythology: The Wessex Novels of John Cowper Powys
Amorous Life: John Cowper Powys and the Manifestation of Affectivity (H.W. Fawkner)
Postmodern Powys: New Essays on John Cowper Powys (Joe Boulter)
Rethinking Powys: Critical Essays on John Cowper Powys
Paul Bowles & Bernardo Bertolucci
Rainer Maria Rilke
Joseph Conrad: *Heart of Darkness*
In the Dim Void: Samuel Beckett
Samuel Beckett Goes into the Silence
André Gide: Fiction and Fervour
Jackie Collins and the Blockbuster Novel
Blinded By Her Light: The Love-Poetry of Robert Graves
The Passion of Colours: Travels In Mediterranean Lands
Poetic Forms

POETRY

Ursula Le Guin: Walking In Cornwall
Peter Redgrove: Here Comes The Flood
Peter Redgrove: Sex-Magic-Poetry-Cornwall
Dante: Selections From the *Vita Nuova*
Petrarch, Dante and the Troubadours
William Shakespeare: *The Sonnets*
William Shakespeare: Complete Poems
Blinded By Her Light: The Love-Poetry of Robert Graves
Emily Dickinson: Selected Poems
Emily Brontë: Poems
Thomas Hardy: Selected Poems
Percy Bysshe Shelley: Poems
John Keats: Selected Poems
D.H. Lawrence: Selected Poems
Edmund Spenser: Poems
Edmund Spenser: *Amoretti*
John Donne: Poems
Henry Vaughan: Poems
Sir Thomas Wyatt: Poems
Robert Herrick: Selected Poems
Rilke: Space, Essence and Angels in the Poetry of Rainer Maria Rilke
Rainer Maria Rilke: Selected Poems
Friedrich Hölderlin: Selected Poems
Arseny Tarkovsky: Selected Poems
Novalis: *Hymns To the Night*
Paul Verlaine: Selected Poems
Arthur Rimbaud: Selected Poems
Arthur Rimbaud: *A Season in Hell*
Arthur Rimbaud and the Magic of Poetry
D.J. Enright: By-Blows
Jeremy Reed: Brigitte's Blue Heart
Jeremy Reed: Claudia Schiffer's Red Shoes
Gorgeous Little Orpheus
Radiance: New Poems
Crescent Moon Book of Nature Poetry
Crescent Moon Book of Love Poetry
Crescent Moon Book of Mystical Poetry
Crescent Moon Book of Elizabethan Love Poetry
Crescent Moon Book of Metaphysical Poetry
Crescent Moon Book of Romantic Poetry
Pagan America: New American Poetry

MEDIA, CINEMA, FEMINISM and CULTURAL STUDIES

J.R.R. Tolkien: The Books, The Films, The Whole Cultural Phenomenon
J.R.R. Tolkien: Pocket Guide
The *Lord of the Rings* Movies: Pocket Guide
The Ghost Dance: The Origins of Religion
Cixous, Irigaray, Kristeva: The *Jouissance* of French Feminism
Julia Kristeva: Art, Love, Melancholy, Philosophy, Semiotics and Psychoanalysis
Luce Irigaray: Lips, Kissing, and the Politics of Sexual Difference
Hélene Cixous I Love You: The *Jouissance* of Writing
Andrea Dworkin
'Cosmo Woman': The World of Women's Magazines
Women in Pop Music
Discovering the Goddess (Geoffrey Ashe)
The Poetry of Cinema
The Sacred Cinema of Andrei Tarkovsky
Andrei Tarkovsky: Pocket Guide
Andrei Tarkovsky: *Mirror*: Pocket Movie Guide
Andrei Tarkovsky: *The Sacrifice*: Pocket Movie Guide
Walerian Borowczyk: Cinema of Erotic Dreams
Jean-Luc Godard: The Passion of Cinema
John Hughes and Eighties Cinema
Ferris Bueller's Day Off: Pocket Movie Guide
Jean-Luc Godard: Pocket Guide
The Cinema of Richard Linklater
Liv Tyler: Star In Ascendance
Blade Runner and the Films of Philip K. Dick
Paul Bowles and Bernardo Bertolucci
Media Hell: Radio, TV and the Press
An Open Letter to the BBC
Detonation Britain: Nuclear War in the UK
Feminism and Shakespeare
Wild Zones: Pornography, Art and Feminism
Sex in Art: Pornography and Pleasure in Painting and Sculpture
Sexing Hardy: Thomas Hardy and Feminism

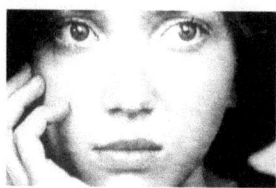

In my view *The Light Eternal* is among the very best of all the material I read on Turner. (Douglas Graham, director of the Turner Museum, Denver, Colorado)

The Light Eternal is a model monograph, an exemplary job. The subject matter of the book is beautifully organised and dead on beam. (Lawrence Durrell)

It is amazing for me to see my work treated with such passion and respect. (Andrea Dworkin)

Sex-Magic-Poetry-Cornwall is a very rich essay... It is like a brightly-lighted box. (Peter Redgrove)

CRESCENT MOON PUBLISHING

www.ingramcontent.com/pod-product-compliance
Lightning Source LLC
Chambersburg PA
CBHW062218080426
42734CB00010B/1936